CAROL BURNETT
MERYL STREEP
ELLEN BURSTYN
LORETTA SWIT
JANE FONDA
MARLO THOMAS

These are some of the women who have seen Alan Alda at his very best—and at times at his worst.

Theirs are some of the candid views offered in a book that searches for the truth behind the immaculate image of the man who has become not only America's #1 star but also one of America's most admired human beings.

All Alda fans (and that means most of us) will want to read the dramatic life-story of this complex, controversial, magnetic, and superbly gifted man—Alan Alda.

ALAN ALDA
AN UNAUTHORIZED BIOGRAPHY

"THE MOST ADMIRED MAN IN AMERICA"
—*Ms. Magazine*

Great Reading from SIGNET

- [ ] **ALAN ALDA: AN UNAUTHORIZED BIOGRAPHY by Jason Bonderoff.** (#AE1419—$2.75)*
- [ ] **FIRST YOU CRY by Betty Rollin.** (#AE1259—$2.50)
- [ ] **SAVE ME THE WALTZ by Zelda Fitzgerald.** (#Y5603—$1.25)
- [ ] **BOGIE by Joe Hyams.** (#E9189—$1.75)
- [ ] **KATE: THE LIFE OF KATHARINE HEPBURN by Charles Higham.** (#AE1212—$2.95)
- [ ] **PENTIMENTO by Lillian Hellman.** (#AE1543—$2.95)
- [ ] **ELEANOR: THE YEARS ALONE by Joseph P. Lash.** (#AE1293—$3.95)
- [ ] **ELEANOR AND FRANKLIN by Joseph P. Lash.** (#AE1231—$4.95)
- [ ] **SINATRA by Earl Wilson.** (#E7487—$2.25)
- [ ] **THE WOMAN HE LOVED by Ralph G. Martin.** (#E9074—$2.50)
- [ ] **THE ROCKEFELLERS by Keith Colher and David Horowitz.** (#E8869—$2.95)
- [ ] **IF YOU COULD SEE WHAT I HEAR by Tom Sullivan and Derek Gill.** (#AE1240—$2.50)
- [ ] **SONG OF SOLOMON by Toni Morrison.** (#AE1446—$2.95)
- [ ] **THREE BY FLANNERY by Flannery O'Connor.** (#E9792—$2.95)
- [ ] **KINFLICKS by Lisa Alther.** (#E9794—$2.95)

*Price slightly higher in Canada

Buy them at your local bookstore or use this convenient coupon for ordering.
THE NEW AMERICAN LIBRARY, INC.,
P.O. Box 999, Bergenfield, New Jersey 07621
Please send me the books I have checked above. I am enclosing $_____
(please add $1.00 to this order to cover postage and handling). Send check
or money order—no cash or C.O.D.'s. Prices and numbers are subject to change
without notice.

Name_____

Address_____

City _____ State _____ Zip Code _____
Allow 4-6 weeks for delivery.
This offer is subject to withdrawal without notice.

ALAN ALDA

AN UNAUTHORIZED BIOGRAPHY
BY JASON BONDEROFF

A SIGNET BOOK

NEW AMERICAN LIBRARY

TIMES MIRROR

SIGNET TRADEMARK REG. U.S. PAT. OFF. AND FOREIGN COUNTRIES
REGISTERED TRADEMARK—MARCA REGISTRADA
HECHO EN CHICAGO, U.S.A.

SIGNET, SIGNET CLASSICS, MENTOR, PLUME, MERIDIAN AND NAL
BOOKS are published by The New American Library, Inc.,
1633 Broadway, New York, New York 10019

First Printing, March, 1982

1 2 3 4 5 6 7 8 9

PRINTED IN THE UNITED STATES OF AMERICA

To Louis Bonderoff,
my father and friend—
no son ever had a better teacher

ACKNOWLEDGMENTS

A number of people shared reminiscences of Alan Alda with me, but I am particularly indebted to actress Patricia Englund, who worked with Alan on *That Was the Week That Was.* The staff of Stepinac High School in White Plains, N.Y., kindly allowed me to view memorabilia from Alan's graduating class; and Stepinac alumnus J. Radley Herold not only contributed his own anecdotes, but helped me contact several of Alan's former teachers and classmates.

Special thanks must go to certain residents of Elmsford, N.Y., who graciously welcomed me into their homes. Without their help, it would have been impossible to recreate a picture of Alan's teenage years.

My longtime friends Bob and Leslie Thornton helped establish contact with other sources in White Plains; Ken Sherber and Cynthia Bostick, of Kacey Associates, provided help with New York and Hollywood sources. I am grateful to typist Nancy Harbour for her patience with the manuscript, and to my co-workers at Sterling's Magazines, Inc., Alice Koenigsberg and Anne Marie McKenna, for editorial help.

My wife Glenna has been my partner on this project —editorially and creatively—from start to finish. Alan Alda says that love comes in waves, but so too does writing. The by-line may be mine, but much of the insight and inspiration is Glenna's.

"... So was it when my life began;
So is it now I am a man;
So be it when I shall grow old ...
The Child is father of the Man ..."
                    —*William Wordsworth*

"His ambition—to follow in the footsteps
of his famous father."
                    —*Caption under Alan Alda's photo*
                    in his high school yearbook, 1952

1

In 1966, Alan Alda stood on a Broadway stage looking like a mutant version of Fabian and Frankie Avalon. He wore a teased black wig, ballet tights and the kind of gaudy shirt that might have come straight from Elvis' closet. The costume—designed to parody a sweaty, arrogant rock singer—was supposed to get laughs, and it did. It also helped Alan win a Tony nomination for his bravura three-character performance in an offbeat musical called *The Apple Tree*.

The show was a trio of one-act variations on the Garden of Eden story. In the first, Alan portrayed the Biblical, bumbling Adam; in the second, he was Sanjar, a barbaric gladiator forced to choose between the Lady and the Tiger; in the final piece he became Flip, the grotesque rock singer. Frankly, Alan hated Flip, even though that role brought him some of his best applause of the evening. He felt foolish in the costume—undignified, a circus spectacle instead of a serious performer.

In fact, one night when *The Apple Tree* was trying out in Boston prior to its New York opening, the black tights and wig just got to be too much for him.

Standing backstage, waiting to go on, he began to remember his student theater days at Fordham University, when he had dreamed of playing roles like Oedipus Rex and Richard II, and had promised himself that someday he'd be the new Olivier. He thought about the years right after college, too. Alan, the struggling young actor, had worked as a clown at gas-station and fried-chicken-store openings. It was the only way he could support his family while he waited for his big break. And what had it all been for? For *this!* So he could dress up and parade on stage, not to recite Shakespeare, but to show off his legs *à la* Marlene Dietrich. Alan, the clown, was still a far cry from Olivier's Hamlet. The stakes were higher—the arena had changed from Amoco stations to Schubert theaters—but in his heart Alan knew the truth: he hadn't made much progress since the days when he had done pratfalls for the customers while Nick the owner cut the ribbon at the gas pump.

As these doubts and insecurities assailed him, Alan stood in the wings crying. He wept awkwardly, as a grown man unaccustomed to tears weeps. Then he pulled himself together quickly—firm, disciplined, in control once more—and walked onstage. But that night in Boston, by making his third-act entrance, he also made a decision that would change his life. For a moment, he'd come frighteningly close to tearing off the costume and deserting the show. But he hadn't. Instead, he opted for the applause, the steady paycheck, the billing after Barbara Harris and Larry Blyden (but still above the title). It wasn't Shakespeare, but it was awfully close to stardom. That night, he gave up the fantasy of greatness for the reality of success.

As Alan wrestled with his conscience backstage in a Boston theater, he thought of his father, too. Sixteen years before—when Alan was just an overweight,

2

wisecracking kid in high school—Robert Alda had been a bona fide matinee idol. After a string of Warner Brothers films, he'd come east to create the role of gambler Sky Masterson in *Guys and Dolls*, a dazzling and memorable Broadway musical. But personally and professionally, *Guys and Dolls* hadn't done as much as one would have thought for Alda senior. Just a few years later—passed over for the screen version of the musical and embroiled in a bitter divorce from Alan's mother—Robert had wound up in Europe making second-rate Italian westerns. In those days, Alan had wept, too, unable to understand his mother's vengeful clutching at alimony and property settlements or his father's seemingly callous absorption in work and pleasure.

But now it was 1966. Alan was married with three children of his own and *The Apple Tree* was coasting into New York with encouraging reviews. With nine years of professional acting under his belt, Alan had survived enough ego blows in show business himself to see his father in a kinder light. He knew the quiet rage that builds in a man whose work is frequently at the mercy of fickle audiences, unscrupulous producers and money-hungry middlemen.

Alan had accumulated his own bag of failures and frustrations: good roles in plays that closed within a week; auditions where you didn't get turned down flat, but you didn't get called back, either; four months on the road; four months in New York; and four months unemployed—the roller-coaster wave of jubilation and despair that every actor rides. And how did it affect your marriage and your mortgage and your children when day after day, year after year, you watched yourself racing around, not *getting anywhere*, while agents, directors and producers kept slicing up another little piece of your insides?

Yes, Alan the actor could finally understand his father, because he'd been there, too. Alan could love him and forgive him, maybe even learn a few pointers from the old man, who'd been through the mill in both Hollywood and New York. Alan, after all, was following the same road his father had taken, even if he was determined not to stumble into the same potholes.

Love and rage . . . isn't that how every son approaches his father? Feeling intimidated on the one hand, infinitely wiser on the other? What a complex web of hopes, grudges, disillusionments and pride each generation of men passes on to the next.

Pop, I need your advice. . . .

Please, Dad, I can do it myself. . . .

Fathers and sons—the eternal conflict. Sigmund Freud would have us believe that all men are doomed to be competitors as long as one man's wife is another man's mother; yet *The Courtship of Eddie's Father* and *Kramer vs. Kramer* naively reassure us that big boys and little boys are really buddies at heart.

Enemies or friends . . . how does it really work? Most men spend a lifetime flexing and testing—imitating, rejecting and reevaluating their paternal legacy. Some men choose to fail to spite their fathers; some men compulsively succeed to dwarf them. In Alan Alda's case, the psychological threads are even finer: for here is the driven son of a driven man; yet, apart from their mutual ambition, in certain ways they are strangers who share the same name. Stardom is the bond that holds them locked together.

Show business, after all, was Alan's birthright. From the beginning, Robert Alda was a fascinating, inspiring character to his son. He was the prime reason that little Allie, who felt more comfortable in a room filled with books than in a room filled with people, learned to memorize jokes, not batting averages. "I never considered any other career," Alan has

4

often said. "I had to be an actor simply because that's what my father was and I idolized him."

Actually, as a child, it was easier for Alan to idolize his father from a distance than to know him up close. In 1936, when Alan was born, Bob Alda was a struggling stage entertainer, often on the road or hanging around the Times Square eateries where fellow comics like Bud Abbott, Phil Silvers and Rags Ragland congregated. He traveled in a raucous, expansive Broadway circle. Even when he wasn't out of town, he was too busy pounding the pavement, hustling for his next vaudeville booking, to classify as an ordinary family man. Allie would just be getting up in the morning when his father would finally be winding down to sleep after doing two shows a night, sixth on the billing at some gaudy burlesque hall where the bumps and grinds, not Bob Alda's rendition of "Roses in December," would lure in the patrons.

But playing second banana in vaudeville was just a weigh station for Bob Alda. Ironically, Alan grew up absorbing two entirely different perspectives on show business. Until the age of seven, he saw his father knocked around from one third-rate strip palace to another; then a Warner Brothers contract—and a movie called *Rhapsody in Blue*—transformed him into an overnight star. The Aldas went from borderline poverty in New York to limousines and caviar in Hollywood. Through his father's eyes, Alan glimpsed both sides of the acting world, failure and success—and by the time he reached adolescence, he knew the dangers of both.

Later on, in the 1950s, Alan would find himself an unwilling spectator in yet a third upheaval in his father's life: Bob Alda's struggle to build a new career when middle age suddenly changed all the rules in the Hollywood game. And Alan would learn from that, too.

5

For if there's any lesson Robert Alda has bequeathed his son, it's the secret of survival. Today, at sixty-seven, the formidable Italian-American actor still cuts a powerful figure in a town that burns up matinee idols at an alarming rate. But Robert Alda has survived it all—Prohibition, WPA projects, Eisenhower's era, the decline and fall of the studio empires—and he's still kicking. If he chose, he could retire and write his memoirs of the borscht circuit and burlesque halls, of his lush Technicolor days in *Cinderella Jones* and *April Showers*, his once-in-a-lifetime triumph in *Guys and Dolls*, or his less than lush days as a host on TV quiz shows and then as a gladiator in *Revenge of the Barbarians*.

But the legend refuses to slip into freeze-frame. Now on the verge of his fiftieth anniversary in show business, Robert Alda lives in Pacific Palisades, California, playing a prominent role on the NBC soap opera *Days of Our Lives* and counting his royalties as co-author with his wife Flora of a best-selling cookbook on pasta.

Alda is a unique archaeological find in the disposable-talent region of Hollywood: neither perenially famous nor sadly forgotten, and far from showing signs of withering like so many of his contemporaries of the 1930s. His hair is silvered, his face weather-beaten, but he is still handsome. The trim physique, the strong voice, the engaging smile—all the pieces of his magnetism are still there, just rearranged by age a little. He hasn't lost the charisma, only the youthfulness, that made him so right as the smooth charmer Sky Masterson thirty years ago.

Perhaps the major difference between then and now is merely a change of billing. In 1951, when *Guys and Dolls* earned him a Tony Award, Alda was at the zenith of his career, so hounded by public acclaim that he installed his family in an isolated house

6

in Elmsford, N.Y., to protect their privacy. The woods kept autograph seekers out, while fifteen-year-old Alan plodded through chemistry and tried to imitate his father's success by writing skits for the drama club at Archbishop Stepinac High School. Today, the tables have turned. Alan earns $2,500,000 a year to film twenty-six episodes of *M*A*S*H*. He wins Emmies and popularity polls as America's premier television actor, appears on the cover of *McCall's*, *Ms.* and *People* magazine in the same month, and has now inked a three-picture independent moviemaking deal with Universal. The senior-class play Alan wrote (and starred in) at Stepinac High grossed $300 in ticket sales. His latest movie, *The Four Seasons* (which he also wrote and starred in), earned a whopping $40 million within a few months after its release. No wonder Robert Alda jokes, "These days I have to make an appointment just to have lunch with my son."

It's a jest that the "old man" utters with affectionate pride. After all, if Alan's success has far outdistanced his own, isn't that what every father wants for his son?

As a kid, Alan saw the frustrations of the entertainer's life, but he also sensed the nobility of purpose underneath it all. One of his earliest memories was of standing backstage at a New York burlesque theater watching his father charm a tired audience into a few moments of pure escape. There was something important and beautiful about giving people the gift of laughter.

Not surprisingly, though, Alan the would-be actor didn't get his father's blessing easily. Considering Papa Alda's long struggle to break out of the vaudeville circuit and his later battles with Hollywood, he had mixed emotions about his son's playing with stage fire. For a long time, he tried to steer Alan into a more secure profession, like medicine. But when Alan

7

came home with a test grade of 10 after his first chemistry final at Fordham University, his father began to soften.

In retrospect, Robert Alda maintains that he purposely played devil's advocate to stiffen Alan's resolve. "He had to want it for himself," Bob explains. "I couldn't want it for him. If I'd tried to ram show business down his throat, he wouldn't have been happy. But once he made his choice, then I did all the encouraging I could, even trying to get producers and directors interested in him. Of course, I saw he had talent. If he didn't have talent, I wouldn't have pushed at all.

"I once told Alan, 'You're the one who has to prove you have staying power. I can only open the door. If you want to stay in that room, you damn well better show them your talent!' And he did."

Alan graduated from Fordham in 1956 and spent the next eight years appearing in summer stock and off-Broadway, hanging on with steely determination—like hundreds of other young actors—and waiting for that elusive big break. It didn't come until 1964, when he was cast as Diana Sands' leading man in the poignant Broadway comedy *The Owl and the Pussycat*. During those frustrating eight years, Papa Alda, navigating some rough career straits of his own, held his peace and let Alan learn his own lessons. "It's hard to give your sons advice," he says. "It's like that old joke, 'It's amazing how smart my father got as he grew older.' I realized that criticism from a stranger, a director or a co-worker, might be a hundred times more valuable than anything coming from me. I was too close to him. Of course, that never *entirely* stopped me from talking." He laughs. "We put things on the table and discuss what we have to. It's always been that way in our family."

Curiously enough, putting things on the table—voicing hurt feelings and emotions—is the theme of Alan's movie *The Four Seasons;* and Jack Burroughs, the character Alan created specifically for himself in the film, seems unable to do that. At one point, his wife Kate (played by Carol Burnett) lashes out at him for never losing his temper, yet underneath never being able to forgive a friend for disappointing him. The fictional Jack Burroughs has a serious problem communicating his anger and his hurt. The question is: Did Alan Alda blend fantasy and truth in creating this film persona for himself?

Outwardly, the film is the story of three middle-aged couples, examining their marriages and the cross-currents of their friendship. The script is deceptively simple. Three New York couples—Alda and Burnett, Jack Weston and Rita Moreno, Len Cariou and Sandy Dennis—make a seasonal ritual out of vacationing together; but a crisis erupts when one of the partnerships hits the skids. Len Cariou, who plays Nick, the disenchanted husband, leaves his neurotic, compulsive wife, Sandy Dennis, for a much younger—and much more appealing—woman played by Bess Armstrong. During the rest of the film, the other couples slowly and painfully learn to accept this change of partners as inevitable, like a change of seasons.

That is, everyone except Alan Alda—who holds out till the last reel of the film. It rankles him that his best friend is a quitter as a husband; in fact, he views Cariou's desertion of Sandy Dennis almost as a personal betrayal.

In an especially poignant scene between the two men, Cariou tries to explain things to Alda. His marriage—to a woman who no longer understands him—has been cold and unloving for years. Even though he's middle-aged, with a grown daughter in college, he wants a chance to start over before it's too late. Bess Armstrong makes him feel young and hopeful again. In fact, he's even thinking of starting a family once they're married. Is it a crime, Cariou asks, to choose happiness over guilt?

In Alda's eyes, yes. These revelations do not draw the two men more tightly together; instead, Alda recoils from this honest confession of middle-aged anguish. He feels no compassion for his friend's plight, no sense of renewed closeness at a private pain shared. To Alda—straitlaced and judgmental—Cariou is a coward for walking out on his marriage, a failure as a man for placing a higher premium on sexual pleasure than on the dictates of conformity.

Low-keyed as this statement is in *The Four Seasons*, it's still a rather emotional departure for the forty-five-year-old *M*A*S*H* star, who scripted and directed the screenplay himself. The theme is more than just "couple has friend—couple loses friend—couple gets friend back." It's really the story of how one man—played by Alan Alda—reacts to another man's midlife turmoil.

Why did this theme intrigue Alda enough to write a major motion picture about it? In a 1979 interview with *New York Post* reporter Curt Davis, Alda said, "It hurts my work if people know an awful lot about my private life. Then they look for that—or the opposite of it—on the screen."

Yet as much as Alan prefers to keep certain parts of his private self hidden from biographical inquiry, one can't help thinking about Robert Alda after seeing *The Four Seasons*. The parallels—man to man, father to son—are so striking that it's hard to believe that Alan simply pulled this story out of thin air. The anguish the characters express is too real, the pain they expose is too intense, not to leave the conviction that Alan was writing from things he felt deeply and sincerely at some point in his life.

Like the character of Len Cariou's Nick, Robert

10

Alda knew his own season of discontent. After more than twenty years of marriage, he left Alan's mother and, very quickly, started over with a much younger woman. Alan was in his junior year at Fordham when the Aldas separated and his father headed for Europe, leaving a wake of emotional and financial problems. In Italy, the forty-one-year-old Alda fell in love with Flora Marino, a young Italian actress; and shortly after their marriage she presented him with a son, Antony.

How Alan reacted to this tumultuous change of seasons in his own family remains unclear; but the script of *The Four Seasons* follows a hauntingly similar pattern. In a climactic moment, newlywed Bess Armstrong—unable to bear the smug disapproval of her husband's friends any longer—throws a monkey wrench into their last vacation together. Late at night, she rushes out of their New England cabin into the freezing temperature alone. Cariou is petrified with fear that she'll injure herself, because she's pregnant. In the final scene, Alda rescues her as she stands on a frozen lake, the whole crew pulling together, their friendship suddenly stronger than any of their petty differences.

In the film, Alan Alda learns to accept a friend who doesn't live up to his own standards of perfection. In reality, it's a role that Alan played opposite his own father.

2

Robert Alda was born Alfonso D'Abruzzo on February 26, 1914, five months before the outbreak of World War I. His father, a barber, had emigrated from Italy at the age of fourteen, and the family lived in a tenement on Manhattan's Lower East Side, right under the Third Avenue elevated train tracks. It was a grimy, brawling, noisy neighborhood, full of immigrants trying to make their way in an alien country, and most of the large D'Abruzzo clan clung together within a few blocks. Alfonso grew up surrounded by a vast network of cousins, aunts, uncles and all their relations by marriage.

Years later, when his first movie, *Rhapsody in Blue,* was about to premiere, he wrote his mother a letter from Hollywood, asking her to arrange a family gathering on his next trip back to New York. She wrote back, apologizing for the fact that she'd only be able to squeeze about three hundred relatives into her apartment. Mama Mia! How could she possibly accommodate the rest of the cousins and in-laws who were sure to show up on the doorstep for a reunion with Alfonso the movie star?

If anything, it was surprise that drew the whole clan together for this homecoming, because Alfonso had always been pegged the black sheep of the family. In those days, there were only two routes for breaking out of the ghetto. A young man could either become a priest or a professional, and Alfonso had turned his back on both avenues of security for a not quite respectable life in show business. His parents hadn't exactly applauded his theatrical ambitions.

Originally, Alfonso had planned on becoming an architect. He studied for two years at New York University, paying his way by working part-time as an apprentice draftsman with a large Manhattan architectural firm. But in 1929, the stock market crashed and the bottom fell out of American life. Hard work and good grades could no longer buy a nickel subway ride, much less a college education. In the early 1930s, when the Depression hit with full force, Alfonso lost his job. Unable to scrape together money for books and tuition, he had to drop out of NYU.

"When I was growing up I'd wanted to be a doctor," he recalls. "Then I transferred all that drive and energy to architecture. I was six months away from my architectural degree when the Depresssion wiped me out. In those days, you were lucky just to be working, and the only job an architect could get was with the WPA—government handouts—because nobody was building anything. Architects were making $24.75 on the WPA payroll. I went into an amateur contest, won first prize singing, and was paid twenty-five dollars. It was a quarter more than an architect's salary, so I said, 'Now I'll go into show business.' "

In college, Alfonso had done a number of amateur musicals and picked up pin money on the bandstand circuit. He'd earn $5 or $10 dollars a night—a lavish sum—singing at weddings and union halls with two of his uncles who had an orchestra. Alfonso's fine tenor voice and dark handsome looks (later, Hollywood publicists would dwell on his vague resemblance to Cary Grant) helped give him natural stage presence. With a college degree suddenly out of reach, singing for his supper seemed a lot more lucrative than selling pencils in Bryant Park, as many of his classmates at NYU were forced to do.

To his parents, a life in beer parlors and burlesque halls was a crazy notion, but they didn't have much chance to object. "I was already married by the time I was nineteen," he recalls, "so I was out of the house making my own decisions, living my own life."

Actually, Alfonso was five months shy of his nineteenth birthday when he married a pretty blond Irish girl named Joan Browne, who was two years his junior. In 1932, the word "disco" hadn't even been invented, so they met in one of the few places where East Side kids could congregate and socialize—the local delicatessen. Joan was on line ordering cold cuts and Alfonso was standing around, joking with some of his neighborhood pals. Still in high school, Joan was already a local beauty contest winner. Alfonso was immediately attracted to her. After an intense courtship, they were married on September 31, 1932.

The bridegroom was starting to earn a reputation as the Rudy Vallee of the Lower East Side, but he realized that his hard-to-pronounce Italian name would never do on a vaudeville marquee. So the first step was to anglicize it. He dropped Alfonso, replacing it with Robert, then combined the first two letters of his first and last names to create Alda. Under his new stage name, he managed to earn $2 a night singing on the *Major Bowes' Amateur Hour* radio show, while clerking in a department store by day.

By 1936, the Depression had eased up a bit. The Aldas, now married three and a half years, were ensconced in a small apartment on East 32nd Street and Third Avenue. Robert's gradually expanding career as a radio singer and a straight man in burlesque had allowed them to make the big jump from the Lower East Side to midtown.

Of course, now more than ever, they needed all the room they could afford, because on January 28, 1936, their son, Alfonso D'Abruzzo, Jr., was born. As an infant, he was dubbed Allie by Bob and Joan and all their Schubert Alley buddies, but later he was enrolled in kindergarten under the more formal but very Americanized name Alan Alda.

In 1936, the breadlines were growing thinner and business was starting to pick up again; still, a lot of impoverished New Yorkers were selling apples in Washington Square. Robert Alda was doing better than most, not sensationally but eking out a living in second-rate burlesque houses in New York and touring the Midwest and Canada on the live-entertainment circuit. Of course, it wasn't a livelihood with much future. With the arrival of talking pictures almost ten years before, vaudeville had waned into a dying medium and burlesque was in even worse shape. The strippers were the real stars of the show, anyway, and second bananas like Bob Alda—who played clowns and stooges and sang sentimental ballads—were only on the bill to keep the customers quiet while the girls changed costumes.

For better or for worse, though, this was the world that Robert Alda traveled in; and it was Allie's first introduction to show business. Bawdy, backbreaking and far from innocent—the theatrical world that Allie glimpsed as a child bore little resemblance to those then-popular Dick Powell–June Allyson movies where ingenues triumphed over disaster and every production was 99 $^{44}/_{100}$ % pure. Robert Alda often brought his son backstage, where uproarious characters like

Rags Ragland and Phil Silvers would take turns baby-sitting while Dad entertained on stage. They were an unforgettable education in themselves.

Rags Ragland, an ex-boxer from Louisville, Kentucky, was six feet five inches tall, and his reputation as a brawler and a ladies' man more than equaled his fame as a Broadway comedian. Ragland spent most of his offstage hours—and his paycheck—drinking and getting into fights. Working with Rags had its hazards, too, especially if he felt he was being upstaged. Once he teamed with a Yiddish dialect comedian who kept stealing his laughs, so Rags taught him a lesson by nailing his shoes to the stage floor. The poor guy couldn't get off the stage until the manager of the theater came and rescued him with a crowbar.

Occasionally, fights broke out between straight men who were dating the same stripper—or even between entertainers and the audience. Hecklers who tried to assault the strippers or interrupt a comic in the middle of his act found themselves bounced out of the theater by the management, if the performers didn't rush off the stage to pounce on them first.

Along with the occasional fireworks, little Allie also saw the fierce camaraderie between the performers, and many of his father's stage cronies became like second family to him. In fact, one of them, Phil Silvers, helped give Allie his first break in show business. When he was six months old, Allie was front row center in the audience, bundled in his mother's arms, while Phil Silvers and Bob Alda were on stage entertaining. In the middle of his routine, Silvers bounded offstage, snatched Allie out of Joan's arms, and made him part of his comedy skit. Blinking sleepily under the lights—and blissfully unaware of where he was—Alan Alda got his first laughs before a live audience.

By the age of three, he'd become a backstage regular; yet Bob and Joan never worried that the bump-and-grind atmosphere might be a corrupting influence on their impressionable toddler. In reality, despite the gaudy legend surrounding burlesque, it was actually a very mild and far from pornographic art form. The ladies on the bill did a lot more teasing than stripping, and most of the off-color jokes went right over a three-year-old's head. To Allie, in fact, the strippers were a pretty ordinary bunch of girls—although they were certainly a lot less reserved than his father's rosary-clutching Italian aunts. Between shows, they'd let Allie hang around their dressing rooms; they were thrilled to be babysitters for the afternoon, and enjoyed a rare chance to act sisterly or maternal. When the time came to change into their show costumes, they simply asked Allie to turn around so he wouldn't see them nude. Of course, few of the girls had read Sigmund Freud, so they didn't know that little boys aren't entirely innocent. Alan swears he never peeked, but he wasn't totally immune to their charms, either.

For young Alan, an even more magical and mysterious haunt was the comic's dressing room. There he could happily lose himself for hours, smearing on greasepaint, trying out baggy pants and fake mustaches, and inventing his own make-believe characters. In many ways, Alan was a lonely youngster—an only child who spent far more time in the company of grown-ups than with kids his own age—and his imagination became his chief means of filling the void. With no one else to entertain him, he'd delight himself by making up funny routines for the outrageous slapstick characters he'd create. He'd sit in front of the dressing-room mirror, barely high enough to see his own reflection in the glass, trying out foreign accents and raucous disguises just like his father did on stage every night.

Alan was totally mesmerized by burlesque—hooked

17

on the fantasy and the flamboyance of it all. He loved standing in the wings observing the musical numbers at close range, especially when his father was master of ceremonies. Hearing the applause, watching his father take bows and keep the show going, night after night, Alan couldn't imagine a more dazzling life. Playing cops and robbers or stickball seemed awfully tame by comparison.

In a recent interview with journalist Carey Winfrey, Alan emphasized his early fondness for burlesque and the indelible mark it left on him. Defending it as a lot more innocent and wholesome than any X-rated film nowadays, he asserted that burlesque was "a wonderful place to learn about the theater, the place where you see both the trick and how the magician does it."

But by the late 1930s, the heyday of burlesque was over and even the best magicians were suffering from a power brownout. Movies were luring away both talent and theatergoers; Hollywood—and a contract with a major studio—was a performer's only hope of survival. In November 1937, when Alan was only twenty months old, the writing was already on the wall. The morning after his father opened in a flashy new revue called *Chest Appeal* at New York's Oriental Theatre, *Variety* warned that the death knell for burlesque was beginning to peal. Bob won praise for his renditions of "Sweet Varsity Sue" and "Cabin of Dreams," but the show itself seemed a tired imitation of all the old sex-and-slapstick formulas.

Even though he was working steadily, Bob Alda was still struggling to find his niche as a performer. Like most singers in burlesque, he couldn't be booked strictly as a vocalist, so his contract usually called for him to double in comedy routines as well. In *Chest Appeal*, he had to play second banana to comedian Hank Henry and star stripper Marjorie Roye, feigning a Russian accent and setting them up for laughs in a silly anti-Stalin skit.

All through the 1930s, Alda was forced to take out-of-town jobs in order to make ends meet. Joan and Alan would often travel with him, living out of suitcases in hotels and sleeping cars, a disruptive lifestyle that probably led to Alan's loneliness and isolation from kids his own age. Traveling from city to city with his parents, Alan developed a strong sense of independence, but a shyness with other children. He found it easier to communicate with grown-ups.

To Alan, Robert Alda's work was glamorous and exciting, but he had little inkling of how unhappy the man he idolized really was. After a decade in show business, Bob felt he was still a nobody, worrying constantly where his next booking would come from, nearly thirty years old and bitterly aware that he hadn't made his mark as a young leading man. More and more, he began to see the West Coast as his only salvation from an endless treadmill of second-rate stage work.

For a long time, Bob had suspected that serious dramatic acting might be his escape route, but he had little experience to base his hunch on. His only test as a serious actor had been an accidental stint at a Catskill resort hotel. A few years before, Bob had been hired for the summer as a singer and emcee, but when he arrived, a new vogue in resort entertainment was sweeping the borscht belt. A young emcee named Moss Hart, who happened to be an aspiring playwright, had recently made a huge hit at a nearby resort by ingeniously staging a Eugene O'Neill production. Suddenly, live drama was the rage at all the hotels, and Alda's boss pushed him into putting on a straight play for the summer patrons. "When I realized I could make myself cry on stage," Bob remembers, "I decided to go into acting all the way. After

19

that, there was no other place to head for than Hollywood."

The Warner Brothers lot in California—three thousand miles from the Aldas' New York apartment—was just a few days' journey by train. But it took Robert Alda far longer than a few days to make his dream come true. It was nearly a decade, filled with frustration and disappointment, before Hollywood came within his reach.

3

In 1943, Warner Brothers was having a great deal of trouble finding a suitable lead for its new screen musical, *Rhapsody in Blue*. Although James Cagney, an established Warners star, had just won an Academy Award for his portrayal of song-and-dance man George M. Cohan in *Yankee Doodle Dandy*, Cagney was too short—and too Irish—to be cast as George Gershwin. No other established leading man happened to be available, so the studio elected to cast an unknown in the role.

A Warner Brothers executive who happened to be visiting New York spotted Robert Alda walking down Broadway and was immediately struck by the young singer's striking resemblance to George Gershwin.

"I thought he was crazy," Bob Alda later confided to journalist Inez Wallace. "He stopped me on the street and almost dragged me into a café and told me he could practically promise me a contract if I'd make a movie test for Warners." That kind of good luck was only supposed to happen in Dick Powell movies, and Alda had serious doubts about his chances of impressing the studio on the basis of such a flimsy encounter. But he'd just finished doing a USO tour, entertaining soldiers at army bases from Maine to Florida, and he was unemployed. "I had nothing better to do," he remembers, "so I figured the Gershwin role was worth a shot."

But Bob's wife, Joan, was more optimistic. She told him, "You're going to get the Gershwin role, I know it! You're going to get it because you're ready for it. Things have always happened when you were ready. Remember?"

Although he had little faith himself in the quality of the routine series of screen tests Warner Brothers put him through, Alda did have faith in his wife's judgment, so he persevered. "Joan always knew," he said. "Once she made up her mind that something was going to happen, it was final as far as she was concerned." Joan started planning their move to California before he'd even been offered a contract.

Joan's faith paid off, and Bob signed a long-term contract with *Rhapsody in Blue* as his debut movie effort. In the early publicity for the film, Warner Brothers insisted that Alda's physical resemblance to Gershwin had nothing to do with signing him. But his final Hollywood screen test for the role took place after a long session with studio makeup man Perc Westmore, who literally transformed the slight resemblance to Gershwin into a lifelike reality. "By the time I walked out of the makeup room for the test," Alda recalled, "I really *was* Gershwin. It was a very strange feeling, looking into the mirror and realizing I'd been transformed into an entirely different person."

Of course, Alda was a singer, not a composer, so before filming actually began, he spent several weeks learning how to play the piano. In the film, the concert piece *Rhapsody in Blue* was actually played by Oscar

Levant, but in all the other piano sequences it really was Alda at the keyboard.

Alda was nervous his first day on the set, but he didn't panic. He kept telling himself, "If I don't play him, who will? Nobody else resembles him." And that assurance saved him from stage fright.

Years later, he admitted, "If it wasn't for George Gershwin, I'd still be knocking on doors. I'll always be grateful."

Everything should have been perfect for the Aldas at this point. Bob had his first role in a movie—a starring role at that—and a contract which promised more to come. And a nervous but efficient Joan had accomplished their move to California with a minimum of fuss.

But three days before Bob was scheduled to start work on *Rhapsody in Blue*, tragedy struck. Seven-year-old Alan began complaining of achiness and soon developed a high fever. His father thought it was simply a severe cold, but Joan suspected something worse. She called in a physician, who quickly diagnosed the symptoms as infantile paralysis.

At that point, the Aldas were living in a small house in Hollywood, but they quickly began searching for larger digs—with a private swimming pool—where Alan could exercise in the water to strengthen his debilitated limbs. What they settled on was a twelve-acre ranch in the heart of the San Fernando Valley. The ten-room, five-bath house was just ten miles from the Warner Brothers lot. But even though Alda's screen contract was lavish compared to his New York earnings, medical bills ran high. So Alda turned the olive groves and fruit orchards surrounding the house into a farming business, lucrative enough to cover taxes and home improvements on the property. Aside from the cost of treatments and home physician's care, the Aldas had to hire a private tutor for Alan, who had to drop out of school for two years.

Although Alan eventually recovered, his bout with poliomyelitis left vivid memories. In a 1979 interview with Sue Edmiston for *McCall's Magazine*, he recalled the night he first took ill. He remembers having a slight headache all that day that grew progressively worse. Then, at night, he was seized with a fit of nausea, but when he went to the bathroom to throw up, his knees suddenly buckled under him and he couldn't stand up.

For a seven-year-old, not being able to keep his footing was the most frightening thing of all. By the next morning, he was so stiff all over that he couldn't even bend his head to drink orange juice. His mother, a tense, high-strung woman by nature, immediately suspected polio. His father, thinking she was just being overprotective, tried to dissuade her.

"My father kept saying it was just a cold and it would pass," Alan recalls. "But my mother wouldn't wait. She called a doctor, and as soon as he examined me, he rushed me to the hospital."

Alan credits his mother with probably saving his life because she recognized the symptoms so quickly. For the next eight months, she also became his round-the-clock nurse as she applied hot packs to his back and limbs to battle the disease. For Alan, the painfulness of the treatment was worse than the pain of polio itself. The hot packs were made from woolen blankets that had been cut into small squares and then folded into triangles like diapers. The packs were then soaked in boiling water. When they were too hot to hold, they were literally dropped on the patient's arms, legs and back, and pinned tight around every muscle, despite the physical pain. The theory was that extreme heat, rigorously applied, would relax the afflicted muscles and prevent permanent deformity. In Alan's case, as in many others, the treatment worked, but the emotional price for both the child and the parents who had to apply the packs was devastating.

To this day, Alan recalls the pungent smell of stinging wet wool with distaste. "But I just felt the physical pain," he says. His parents would carry a different, and much deeper, set of scars for the rest of their lives. "They had to hear this kid they loved screaming. They had to keep making me hurt because they knew if they gave in to my cries, if they skipped one single treatment and didn't drop the packs on me every hour, there was every chance I'd remain crippled for the rest of my life."

Later on, Alan became fascinated with the story of Sister Elizabeth Kenny, the Australian nurse who defied the medical profession by promoting this unique form of therapy for infantile paralysis. Until Sister Kenny discovered otherwise, orthodox medicine preached that polio deadened the nerve endings in the afflicted muscles. Patients in the acute stage of the disease were placed in splints, unable to move. Sister Kenny argued that it was the splints—not polio itself—that caused permanent deformity. She argued that polio didn't deaden muscle tissue, it just put the muscles into a state of spasm, and that if heat was applied immediately to relax the afflicted muscles, the spasms would ease and the muscles might function normally again.

It was a treatment she had discovered accidentally, when she was called in to tend an Australian farm girl shortly before World War I. Kenny, who'd never seen a case of polio before, assumed the girl was afflicted with muscle spasms and realized that heat might be the solution. With no doctor on hand to prevent her from following her own instincts, she heated salt in a frying pan, poured it into a bag and put it on the girl's leg. That didn't stop the spasm, so she tried applying a poultice of linseed meat, also to no avail. Finally, out of desperation, she tore up a blanket, dipped it in scalding water, wrung out the strips and placed them on the girl's arms and legs. Her spasms eased immediately, and after a few days she was able to walk again.

Over the years, Sister Kenny successfully treated thousands of paralysis victims, but she remained a pariah in the medical world because she dared to question long-held misconceptions about the nature of polio. In her autobiography, *And They Shall Walk*, she wrote sadly: "I was wholly unprepared for the extraordinary attitude of the medical world in its readiness to condemn anything that smacked of reform or that ran contrary to approved methods of practice." Eventually, though, after many years of ridicule and slander, her success record became undeniable. While most polio victims treated with splints wound up condemned to wheelchairs or iron lungs, children who followed her regimen of hot packs, water baths and exercise—as early as possible—usually recovered full use of their limbs. By 1946, not very long after Alan was struck down by the dread disease, her worldwide recognition was so complete that Hollywood had even released her life story in a screen version starring Rosalind Russell.

Thankfully, by the time Alan was struck down, Sister Kenny's treatment was popular enough for his mother to know what had to be done without wasting precious time. Alan was grateful for his mother's resourcefulness, but later on, the more he investigated Sister Kenny's life, the angrier he became. He felt he owed his own recovery to two women—his mother, who nursed him back to health, and the gifted Australian nurse, whose program of therapy she religiously forced him to follow. But Alan began to see that if the care of polio victims had been left to the men of the world, there might have been no hope for kids like himself. As he read the story of her lonely fight—one determined woman repudiated by the male-dominated medical profession in both Australia and the United States—he felt his first twinge of sympathy for women's rights. For years, because Sister Kenny was a nurse, doctors had refused to investigate her treatment. It was blind, ignorant sexism—especially despicable because it was fostered by supposedly learned men—that kept "hot packs" from being publicized and accepted in the world's leading hospitals. Alan wondered angrily, if Sister Kenny had been a man, would her style of treatment have taken thirty years to gain credence. Probably not.

During his two years at home, Alan had time to ask himself other, deeper questions about definitions of masculinity and femininity. Boys, he knew, were expected to play competitive sports and flex their muscles; but what if a boy remained partially crippled for the rest of his life? Would it make him less of a man? Certainly not. He began to realize that perhaps there was a lot less difference between men and women than anyone dared let on. Elizabeth Kenny was as smart as any man he could think of—and some of the great male writers were as sensitive and emotional as any woman. It was an important and surprisingly mature observation for a nine-year-old boy. While other boys his age were engaged in playing ball, climbing trees and other physical activities, Alan was restrained from exploring the world around him. Instead, Alan's concept of himself as a man was forced to take root entirely in his mind, strengthening his sensitivity and compassion, traits too often considered exclusively feminine.

During his two-year convalescence, Alan spent

much time paddling around the family swimming pool, slowly regaining the use of his stricken muscles. His imagination was his only friend and ally. He became a voracious reader and even tried his hand at writing. He returned to school academically advanced for his age, but perhaps emotionally alienated from most of his classmates.

4

Somewhat overweight and totally inept at sports, Alan—the new kid at school—didn't fit in easily. More and more, books became his closest companions, and he developed a glib, wisecracking attitude on the surface to cover up his feelings of loneliness and insecurity underneath. As a teenager, Alan didn't have much chance to hang around his father's world, either. Working for Warner Brothers was a vastly different life from doing vaudeville and burlesque. It was a rare treat—not a regular routine—for Alan to accompany his now-famous dad inside the studio gates.

Moreover, Bob Alda was working constantly now, leaving in the early hours of the morning, coming home tired at night, only to immerse himself in the next day's script. After the success of *Rhapsody in Blue*, Alda emerged as a national screen figure, pursued by columnists and fan magazines, an idol whose presence was required at parties and film premieres—at Ciro's and the Brown Derby. But Alda soon discovered that in spite of the glamorous trappings, he was really just a studio workhorse. He made ten films in six years—*Cinderella Jones, Cloak and Dagger, The Man I*

Love, The Beast with Five Fingers, Nora Prentiss, April Showers, Homicide, Hollywood Varieties, Tarzan and the Slave Girl and *Mr. America.*

His studio years were profitable, but creatively less and less rewarding. After seven years in Hollywood, Alda was still waiting for a decent dramatic role that would lift him out of the kind of commercial pap he was constantly entangled in. He grew increasingly vocal about the quality of the film scripts that Warner Brothers offered him during his term of residence there. Alda felt caught in a stranglehold. Even when a good offer came through from another studio, such as Paramount, Warner Brothers wouldn't release him, anxious to keep him on hold in case they needed his services on short notice.

Realizing that his film future might be shaky, Alda prudently began to invest his motion-picture earnings in other ventures. The food business had always intrigued him, and so in the late 1940s, Alda decided to open the kind of eatery that looked promising in ultra-automotive California—a drive-in hamburger joint. He used his architectural background to cut costs by designing the restaurant building himself and even personally supervised the construction. According to a newspaper account of his foray into the brave new world of fast-food chains, once the grills were humming on all burners, he expected to "sit back and count the profits."

But "sitting back" had never really been Alfonso D'Abruzzo's style. So, while continuing to churn out soap operas, he also began trying his hand at live theater in Los Angeles—tackling straight dramatic roles in both revivals and new productions, polishing up his stage acting in case a really big opportunity materialized.

In 1950, it did. Frank Loesser and Abe Burrows cast Alda in their new Broadway-bound musical *Guys and Dolls.* Based on Damon Runyan's classic short stories about gambling life in New York, *Guys and Dolls* starred Sam Levene and Vivian Blain as Nathan Detroit, a comic sharpie, and Adelaide, his long-suffering girlfriend. Alda and Isabel Bigley handled the romantic leads as gambler Sky Masterson and Sarah Brown, the young Salvation Army innocent who fell hopelessly in love with him. At that point, Alda was so disenchanted with Hollywood that it didn't take him long to accept the role. Many years later, recalling his decision to head back east, he told *TV Guide* editor Dwight Whitney, "I was Tiffany's, but they kept putting me in Woolworth's window." *Guys and Dolls*—a priceless gem of a musical even in an era when Rodgers and Hammerstein, Cole Porter and Irving Berlin were all lighting up the Great White Way—finally gave Alda a chance to put his talents on display in something more than a five-and-dime store setting. *Guys and Dolls* opened to rave Broadway reviews and SRO box-office business in November 1950. Alda and the rest of the leads took turns winning every theater award that New York had to offer that season.

According to Broadway legend, Robert Alda wasn't the producers' first choice to play Sky Masterson. Tony Martin, a popular nightclub and recording artist, had been under consideration, while Ethel Merman and Frank Sinatra had both been wooed unsuccessfully to play the other leads (Sinatra eventually did portray Nathan Detroit in the film version). During its pre-Broadway run, the show suffered from other problems aside from casting troubles. Two other writers exhausted their talents before Abe Burrows was called in to perform major script surgery. Backers were nearly ready to demand their money back when he finally fashioned a coherent stage piece out of this sentimental assortment of gamblers, showgirls and Salvation Army missionaries.

Because of the casting and script difficulties, many observers expected *Guys and Dolls* to limp onto Broadway. Instead, it opened on November 24, 1950, at New York's 46th Street Theatre a resounding hit. The next morning, Brooks Atkinson—the dean of American theater critics—started off his review in the *Times* with the announcement "Out of the pages of Damon Runyon, some able artisans have put together a musical play that Broadway can be proud of," then went on to call it a "gutsy" and "uproarious" evening of entertainment. Audiences soon discovered that one of the great pleasures of *Guys and Dolls* was Frank Loesser's charming and memorable score; and Robert Alda, as the romantic lead, got to sing five of the best numbers—"I'll know," "My Time of Day," "If I Were a Bell," "I've Never Been in Love Before," and "Luck Be a Lady Tonight." Singling out Alda's performance, Atkinson wrote, "Robert Alda keeps the romance enjoyable, tough and surly."

Still, the move back east—after seven years in the San Fernando Valley—meant another family upheaval. Bob, Joan and Alan had all grown so accustomed to ranch-style living in California that the thought of settling into a Manhattan apartment didn't hold much appeal. Although it meant a long and tiring commute to Broadway every night, Alda insisted on finding a place where his wife and son could be surrounded by trees instead of asphalt. After much searching, he rented a sprawling old house in Elmsford, N.Y., halfway up New York's posh Westchester County. There the residences were far enough apart to afford peace and privacy, yet, much to Alda's liking, the local village boasted an old-fashioned Italian delicatessen and a high percentage of paisans.

Alan's mother, who'd remained a devout Catholic through all their years in Hollywood, insisted that Alan continue his parochial education, and that fall his parents enrolled him in Archbishop Stepinac High School in nearby White Plains. An all-boys academy, Stepinac High was only two years old and located in a spanking new building on Mamaroneck Avenue near the Scarsdale–White Plains border. In 1948, when the school had first opened its doors, the Cold War was heating up; America—on the brink of the McCarthy era—was busy hunting down Communist sympathizers in every nook and cranny. Perhaps as a result of the rampant anti-Communist fever in White Plains, the school was named after Archbishop Stepinac, a Yugoslav prelate who'd been imprisoned during the Communist takeover in Eastern Europe, although the city of White Plains itself had only a small Slavic population in comparison to Italians and Irish Catholics.

The school was run by priests, and the first graduating class in 1951 boasted 143 students. According to J. Radley Herold, now a White Plains attorney, who was one year ahead of Alan at Stepinac, "Discipline was tough, but corporal punishment was rare. Students who misbehaved in class were given detention—or 'jug' as everyone called it—which meant you were kept after school for an hour or so. A few priests did mete out hand punishment with a ruler, but we kind of expected it. When you're a boy in a Catholic school that kind of goes with the territory."

Undoubtedly, Alan probably spent a few afternoons at Stepinac in "jug," because he developed quite a reputation as a class clown during his junior and senior years there.

Monsignor Paul McDermott, who was on the Stepinac faculty in those days, remembers Alan as "glib, very active in school affairs and full of wisecracks."

Ironically, it was his unacceptable behavior at Stepinac that launched Alan's dramatic career. The Rev. Bernard McMahon, who taught Alan and his best friend, Joe Colangelo, English in their junior year, had despaired of ever getting them to tone down their running comedic commentary in class. He finally decided to try a different tack rather than the usual brand of punishment. He told them to stop wasting their best material in class and write a skit for the school assembly program instead.

As collaborators, Alda and Colangelo were such a hit that they spent the following summer writing an entire original musical called *Love's the Ticket*. The all-student show, which was presented at Stepinac Auditorium in the fall of Alan's senior year, grossed $300 in ticket sales—a far cry from what his father's show, *Guys and Dolls*, was grossing on Broadway every week, but a rather creditable success for an untried young dramatist.

By then, Alan had already decided to follow in his father's footsteps. In his first semester at Stepinac, he became a guiding force of the student drama club and starred in its very first production, called *It Won't Be Long Now*. Since the student body at Stepinac was all-male, seniors and juniors from Good Counsel Academy, the local girls' Catholic high school, were recruited for the female parts. The girls were all members of the Peg-O Dramatic Club at Good Counsel.

Although his father was a Broadway and Hollywood star, Alan didn't ask—or receive—any special treatment in the Stepinac Dramatic Society. "To us, he was just Alan the high school student," J. Radley Herold recalls. "The only thing special I remember was that once he got house seats for us all to go see *Guys and Dolls*. The whole dramatic society went

34

down to New York with the priest who was our faculty adviser."

The 1952 edition of the Stepinac senior-class yearbook, *The Shepherd*, reveals much about young Alan Alda and the inner life of the two-story brick building on Mamaroneck Avenue where he spent some of his most formative years. The Class of '52 dedicated their yearbook to Francis Cardinal Spellman of New York, who is credited as the school's founder; and the following page commemorated Archbishop Aloysius Stepinac, the Yugoslav prelate who'd been imprisoned by the Communists. It's obvious just from a quick glance through the yearbook how deeply the Class of '52 had been impressed by the events of the Korean War and the rising tide of McCarthyism. *Amoris Patriae* ("love of country") was part of the permanent motto engraved on the school's insignia, and the student-written dedication page to Archbishop Stepinac patriotically reminded fellow classmates that the world's current freedom fighters, straining to break the yoke of atheism and totalitarianism, were no less saintly than the early Christian martyrs.

Alphabetically, Alan's name appeared first on the senior-class roster. In *The Shepherd*, he was listed by his full name, Alphonse Joseph Alda, a resident of Elmsford, and a member of the parish of Our Lady of Mount Carmel. Alan's yearbook photo was hardly the picture of a future television idol. Looking distinctly uncomfortable in a nondescript suit, white shirt and tie, Alan's forced smile had the usual nervous quality that everybody cringes over when looking back at it years later.

By the time he was a senior, Alan had slimmed down considerably from his earlier chunkiness, and his features had already begun to mature, making him appear somewhat older than his sixteen years.

But the brush cut of his dark head of hair still looked as if it had been mowed by the local barber. It practically stood up on end, making Alan look as if he'd just received the fright of his life. Years later, critic Rex Reed would remark that Alan Alda reminded him of Henry Aldrich on speed. In his high school graduation picture, Alan looked like a petrified Henry Aldrich.

Under Alan's picture in the yearbook, a small paragraph capsulized his accomplishments and ambitions: "Al will be remembered for the leading part he had in developing Stepinac dramatics. His creative talents impressed our music, script and direction. His ambition—to follow in the footsteps of his famous father."

Running down the list of graduating seniors, the other career choices expressed in *The Shepherd*—attorney, doctor, professional basketball player—were all far more routine adolescent fancies than Alan's rather self-assured notion of Broadway stardom.

Sports was an integral part of Stepinac's extracurricular life, and the school boasted varsity teams in football, baseball, basketball, tennis, track, golf and bowling. There was even a student rifle club—plus an all-male cheerleading squad consisting of nine Stepinac boys who didn't fill out their sweaters nearly as well as the girls from Good Counsel, but who tried hard to make up for it with their raucous enthusiasm. For nonathletic students, there were less hazardous activities like the German Glee Club and the special mission to the Cardinal McCloskey children's home. McCloskey, a Catholic-run orphanage, was situated right next door to Stepinac High, and a number of Stepinac boys served as part-time big brothers to the foundling kids at McCloskey.

During Alan's stint in high school, football still dominated academic life. In 1952, the Crusaders proudly smashed almost every other school on the gridiron, trouncing St. Xavier, Iona, Ossining and Mount St. Michael. Their only stunning defeat came from Cardinal Hayes High School, a tough bunch of football players from the Bronx, who bested Stepinac 13-0.

Sixteen years later, Alan might have had an easier time filming *Paper Lion* if he'd thrown himself to the gridiron wolves back at Stepinac, but he shied away from athletic competition. Instead, he spent his after-school hours guiding the drama club and working on *The Crusader*, the school newspaper, where Alan and his friend Joe Colangelo both served on the literary staff.

Under Alan's aegis, the drama club's productions were such a resounding smash that the Class of '52 devoted two full pages in *The Shepherd* to photographs and reminiscences about the SRO school theater season. The drama club curtain had first gone up that semester with an original turkey-day show called *Lost Thanksgiving*, scripted by Alan Alda and Joe Colangelo. For the annual Yuletide pageant, a more traditional dramatic piece, *Christmas in the Marketplace*, was chosen; but Alda and Colangelo—now affectionately known as Stepinac's answer to Kaufman and Hart—unveiled their ultimate masterpiece, *Love's the Ticket*, that spring.

Alan and Joe had begun working on the script the summer before, and fellow senior Bob Gormley collaborated with them on the musical score. In the warm weather, the three guys held a lot of their writing conferences on the front steps or back playing fields of Stepinac, where the ever-present smell of lilacs in bloom permeated all their work sessions. Years later, Alan recalled that when he sat down at home in Leonia, N.J., to write his first episode of *M*A*S*H*, the smell of lilacs blooming on Mamaroneck Avenue

37

still haunted him. In fact, the sense memory remains so strong, Alan jokes, that he still conjures up lilacs—and the voice of Father McMahon urging him to stop wasting his talent on wisecracks and to write plays—whenever he heads for the typewriter today.

The students played all the parts, built the scenery, painted the backdrops and rang up the receipts for *Love's the Ticket*. The production was personally directed by Father McMahon; and Norma Korn, Jackie Vitucci and a carload of other girls from Good Counsel pitched in on stage and behind the scenes. The show boasted everything from a modern ballet sequence to a soft-shoe number, with an all-boys chorus line in tuxedos, that brought the house down. The big ensemble number was a song called "See Paree" with the Eiffel Tower and Montmartre painted on the backdrop, while Joe Colangelo and Jackie Vitucci got a special ovation for harmonizing on "Hey, World, We're in Love."

Even his father's toast-of-the-town reviews in *Guys and Dolls* couldn't top the glowing notices that classmates bestowed on Alan Alda for *Love's the Ticket*. *The Shepherd* immortalized the production in Stepinac history by recording that "the genuine approval of the critics and the warm applause of the audiences justified the five months' labor in the perfecting of the acting, singing, and dancing."

All the lost time—when Alan and the rest of the drama group had shown up not quite prepared for Latin recitation and chemistry exams—had been worth it. Alan Alda, producer, writer and budding star, had pulled off his first smash hit.

It was a heady kind of success for both Alan and Joe Colangelo, who was one grade behind at Stepinac. If Alan had earned a varsity letter, clobbering the Ossining star quarterback on the five-yard line, he couldn't have emerged a bigger man on campus. At the opening-night cast party that followed all the curtain calls he took for *Love's the Ticket*, Alan was a hero, dancing one slow dance after another with his fellow thespians from Good Counsel, while Patti Paige and Dinah Shore records crooned in the background.

Despite the fact that Stepinac was an all-boys school—and discipline was tough—the Class of '52 didn't exactly lead a monastic life. There were regular school celebrations—the biggest of the year on St. Viator's Day, patron saint of the school's Viatorian fathers. There were also dances, rallies and proms. In the spring of 1951, at Alan's junior prom, the theme was "April Showers," which took its cue not only from the popular Tin Pan Alley song, but from the 1948 motion picture that had, coincidentally, starred Robert Alda.

On social occasions like these, Alan generally wore a polkadot bow tie, white shirt and dark suit, de rigueur attire for the fashion-conscious Stepinac guy in those days. The kids chatted about television and brand-new shows like *I Love Lucy*, the *Milton Berle Texaco Star Theater*, and *Sid Caesar's Your Show of Shows*. Big news on campus was also who had a television set and who didn't, since the medium was still in its infancy and, even in well-to-do Westchester, radio listening and going to the movies were still more popular—and affordable—pastimes.

There was a high political awareness among the Stepinac kids, too. Republicanism predominated, and most seniors were rooting for General Dwight Eisenhower to trounce Democrat Adlai Stevenson in the coming Presidential election. Harry Truman, never a local favorite, had fallen into even lower esteem at Stepinac after hastily firing beloved General Douglas MacArthur as Far Eastern Commander in Chief. "In those days at Stepinac," a fellow alumnus of Alan's recalls, "you were either pro-MacArthur or anti-MacArthur, and that debate generated a lot of heat among the student body. Most of the 'in' kids were fervent supporters of containing Communism and keeping America safe for democracy. Like our parents, we all wanted to see Eisenhower win so we could wrap up the war in Korea quickly and get on with the business of peace. Maybe we all wanted the Korean War over quickly because we didn't want to have to worry about the draft ourselves."

It was during his stay at Stepinac that Alan lived through America's involvement in Korea; and though he kept a cool distance from the kids who were organizing peace rallies and daring to flaunt Stevenson for President buttons, his personal views were already decidedly liberal and quietly antimilitary.

Artistically, Stepinac was a wonderful place for Alan to spend his adolescence, and the drama club gave him a place to assert himself creatively, make friends, become a leader, and escape from the rapidly worsening situation between his parents at home. But Stepinac, in some ways, was also a very safe and antiseptic world, too. His classmates came, almost exclusively, from the better neighborhoods of Westchester—rich suburbs like Scarsdale and Mamaroneck or upper-crust addresses in White Plains. It's hard to find a single black face among the boys in Alan's graduating class; in fact, he finished high school two full years before the Supreme Court ever declared segregation unconstitutional, and then only for public, not parochial, institutions. Civil rights was not high on the list of student priorities in 1952.

Today, if Alan returned to Stepinac, he'd probably be surprised by some of the changes that have taken place since his enrollment there. While the school still maintains a dress code, brush cuts and bow ties have given way to blue jeans and more casual attire for after-school activities. Portraits of Cardinal Spellman and Archbishop Stepinac are still framed in the main lobby, but the picture of a new mentor—Pope John Paul II—now joins them. A huge poster, hand-lettered by the student "Youth for Life" committee, catches every eye that enters Stepinac. It reads: "They used to call it murder—now they call it abortion and it's legal."

Thirty years ago, when Alan was enrolled there, student life was obviously a lot tamer. Social and political questions took a back seat to more immediate concerns. Since Stepinac was practically a brand-new school, struggling to gain a reputation for itself in the academic world, the faculty fathers were constantly trying to build school spirit. Whether it was competing for college scholarships or trying to shape up a school football team, the watchword became *Stepinac First!* Years later, though, at an alumni reunion dinner, a former faculty member joked that all through those early years, while the priests were publicly keeping records of the first student to score a touchdown or win a National Merit Award for Stepinac, they were privately keeping records of the first student to use the urinal or break a window.

Underneath their tough armor, Alan's teachers had a humanity and sense of humor to counteract their strictness. Although privately they didn't take their cries for *Stepinac First!* too seriously, little did they realize that one of their first graduates would make history for the school. Alan Alda, a graduate of the class of 1952, would become a major Hollywood star, as would Jon Voight, a fellow alumnus who entered Stepinac a few years after Alan left.

Alan Alda, self-admittedly, isn't a practicing Catholic.

"It doesn't matter," one alumnus says, "Alan is a responsible family man. He's been married to the same

41

woman for twenty-four years; he's a good father; and his films promote family life. It doesn't matter if he goes to church; he does Stepinac proud in the way he lives."

5

During his years at Stepinac, Alan—like all his class-mates—received Catholic instruction regularly. In religion class, he learned that marriage is a sacrament, that the holy bond between a man and a woman is a lifelong commitment, for the vows that a couple recite on their wedding day are made in the presence of God. Marriage is a promise that cannot be broken.

Although Alan never became a rigorous Catholic himself, he has, over the past twenty-four years, treated his own marriage very much like a sacrament. It may be one of the few parts of his training at Stepinac that made a true impression on him; or, more likely, it may be that his own fidelity to marriage is a reaction against the private turmoil that he saw his parents endure.

For all through his years at Stepinac, while Alan heard the priests over and over again rail against the sinfulness of divorce, he returned home from school each day to see his parents' relationship steadily deteriorating into a state of total alienation.

He watched his father become an increasingly unhappy man. Robert Alda stayed with *Guys and Dolls* for only twenty-two months. In September 1952, he was succeeded on Broadway by Norwood Smith. In the first national touring company, Alda's role went to Allan Jones, father of another future show-business star, too—singer Jack Jones.

Robert Alda had hoped that *Guys and Dolls* might be his ticket back to renewed prominence in Hollywood. But even after his success as Sky Masterson, his film career didn't pick up steam. Perhaps his sorest disappointment was losing the screen version to Marlon Brando, who couldn't sing a note but was considered far more bankable at the box office.

After his stint in *Guys and Dolls* had run its course, Alda decided to try his luck in Europe—alone. The accumulated years of career frustration had fueled his growing estrangement from his wife and undermined the closeness they had once shared to a point where the marriage was unsalvageable. With Alan now enrolled in Fordham University, Robert felt that his son was old enough to accept the separation and survive his father's departure.

Friends and neighbors of the Aldas in Elmsford recall how different from—and distant toward—each other Robert and Joan had seemed when they had first moved to Westchester in 1950. Robert, gregarious and charming, made friends in the area easily, but Joan seemed frightened and withdrawn. The large house they'd rented was on the outskirts of town, isolated and totally surrounded by woods, which only added to her feelings of insecurity. With Robert commuting daily to Broadway and not returning home till well after midnight, she was alone most of the time.

One of the few friends she made in the area was the owner of the local delicatessen and his son. Joan often called on them to help cater the lavish parties that Robert gave for his show-business cronies, but she also relied on them to solve other problems that arose, like fixing the plumbing and repairing the roof. With an absentee husband and a teenage son who spent long days at Stepinac High School rehearsing with the drama club, Joan felt helpless and abandoned. Once she phoned the delicatessen frantic because she'd gotten something in her eye and didn't know how to remove it. She was so upset that the owner's son had to leave a storeful of customers waiting and drive out to the house to calm her down.

The house the Aldas rented in Elmsford was totally enclosed by woods. It was set back perhaps a quarter of a mile from the road with no neighbors on either side close enough to call in an emergency. The nearest building was the local public high school, but since Alan attended Stepinac ten miles away, the Aldas had no contact with Elmsford High, their only neighbor.

The house—a dingy gray brick on the outside, but rambling, spacious and comfortable within—had originally been owned by a well-to-do local banker named Nathan. He lived in such aristocratic style that few townspeople ever called him by his first name; but despite the fact that he lived a notch above them, he was a beloved old figure to most of the residents, famous for returning from his annual winter health pilgrimage to Florida with gifts of oranges and grapefruit for the Elmsford storeowners.

In his later years, Nathan married his secretary, and after his death she rented out the house to Robert and Joan Alda. Joan, who was already becoming somewhat reclusive, immediately fell in love with the privacy of the place and urged Robert to buy it. For two years, he negotiated on and off with Mrs. Nathan, offering her more and more money to sell him the house, but in the end she turned the Aldas down and the property went to a local man and his family. By that time Alan was in Fordham, and Bob was tired of suburban living and commuting anyway, so rather than look for another house in the area, the Aldas moved back to New York.

When they left, hardly anyone in Elmsford missed the Aldas. Joan had been such a quiet woman and Bob had been in New York so much of the time that they'd never really become an integral part of the community. One storeowner's wife remembers that Joan was polite and kindly, but that she usually preferred to call in her orders and have them delivered, rather than doing her shopping in person. Joan was so subdued, and the years had changed her so much, that it seemed hard to believe that she'd once been Miss New York and a contender for the Miss America crown. In Elmsford, she was known as a very religious woman; she spent most of her time outside the house visiting Our Lady of Mount Carmel Church or conferring with the Catholic fathers at Stepinac about her son's education. "She was always having the priests over for dinner," a local merchant recalls, "and on those occasions she used to plan the menus with special care." Joan never missed Sunday mass at Our Lady of Mount Carmel, usually with Alan in tow. But Bob's church attendance became increasingly irregular as he began spending more and more weekends in the city—alone.

Although she kept mainly to herself, Joan's overprotectiveness as a mother was soon obvious to everyone in town. Perhaps because Alan had suffered from polio as a child, she worried about him constantly, monitoring his health, his schoolwork, and the company he kept. It wasn't an easy burden for a sixteen-year-old boy to bear. There was a long, steep drop into the woods right outside the Aldas' property, and Joan fretted that Alan might stumble and kill himself if he came home after dark. Full-time domestic help was another problem. Bob and Joan kept a live-in butler

46

and housekeeper on staff, but hiring new people sent Joan into a tizzy. The butler's bedroom was near Alan's and she used to worry that she'd accidentally hire a criminal—a degenerate or even a murderer who'd slip into Alan's room some night and slit his throat.

Her fears were so strong that even when Alan was sixteen, she refused to let him spend a single night in the house alone. When the Aldas' show-business friends invited them to parties in the city, Bob would wind up staying in the city alone because Joan refused to go. She felt that it was her place as a mother to stay home with her son, even though Alan would probably have been glad to help her pack her bags for the weekend. Bob, on the other hand, loved to party with his Broadway cronies; in fact, Bob's wardrobe of suits and shirts was so lavish that the Aldas' bedroom had wall-to-wall closets filled with Bob's stylish outfits. Joan avoided entertaining his friends at home, as best she could, but she couldn't stop her husband from hanging out in Sardi's after the curtain came down on *Guys and Dolls* at night, or from booking a hotel room in the city on weekends. But when he was gone, her fearfulness only increased. She saw shadows in the woods at night and worried that an intruder might break in. Despite the fact that Alan was with her, and usually one or two live-in domestics, Joan never felt quite safe. Whenever Bob was away, the Elmsford police were put on alert to patrol the area around the Alda house every hour, around the clock.

Apparently, Alan's bout with polio had left her permanently anxious about his health. She developed an avid interest in nutrition and would send delivery boys to the nearest health-food store in White Plains to stock up on vitamins and special enriched delicacies. But fortifying Alan's diet couldn't prevent an occasional scrape or bruise. One time Alan broke a tooth and the local dentist in town wanted to perform an extraction. Joan wouldn't hear of it. She pulled Alan out of high school for a few days and flew back to California with him, so her former dentist could treat him. Although Bob scoffed at the time and expense, Joan felt her overprotectiveness was justified when the dentist in California miraculously saved the tooth.

Aside from the few local merchants who befriended her and the parish priests who were her closest confidants, Joan's only visitor was her younger sister, who came up often from New York. The Aldas rarely entertained show-business personalities, because Joan was growing more and more uncomfortable in Bob's world, but she tried hard to keep her husband home by excelling as a very domestic suburban matron. Once Joan arrived at the local butcher shop with pen and notebook in hand and asked the butcher's Italian wife to teach her how to cook "old-country" style. She wanted to learn how to make all her husband's favorite boyhood dishes.

Joan was apparently happy to live in suburban seclusion, planning menus, making sure that Alan was well cared for, directing servants, and following her religion faithfully. She was content as long as she didn't have to involve herself in the public appearances demanded by her husband's career. Once Bob had agreed to attend a massive bond drive for Israel, along with other top New York and Hollywood stars, at Madison Square Garden. But at the last minute he had to drop out. Rather than let his two tickets go to waste, he gave them to the delicatessen owner's son. When the young man and his steady girl arrived at Madison Square Garden, they were announced over the public address system as "Mr. and Mrs. Robert Alda," then escorted to prominent seats directly behind Gloria Swanson. "I was so embarrassed," Bob's stand-in recalls, laughing, "I didn't know whether to hide under my seat, run out of the place, or stand up and take a bow!".

On another occasion, the Aldas created a sensation by phoning the local grocery store at one in the morning. The groggy-eyed owner answered the phone in near panic because his teenage daughter still hadn't returned from a date, and he was sure it was the police calling to inform him she'd been in a car wreck. But it was only Bob Alda asking if he could have a carload of assorted cold cuts, beer and soda delivered up to his place in a hurry because he'd brought home Milton Berle and a few other show-business pals for an after-the-show get-together.

Later on, when Bob was finishing his run in *Guys and Dolls,* he even tried to lure some of the local paisans into becoming Broadway angels. Bob was considering producing and starring in a brand-new musical called *Herald Square,* and he was looking for financial co-investors. But somehow the project never got off the ground.

To this day, Bob is remembered by the townspeople as outgoing and generous, but nonetheless a rather formal man who kept his distance from folks. "There was a big difference between Alan Alda and his father," one resident recalls. "Robert was always very stiff—he had a certain gallantry, almost. He was a real Broadway type, very sharp clothes, a little bigger than life, but definitely aloof. Alan was always just a very regular guy, your average next-door neighbor's son. Everybody loved that kid."

Alan spent most of his time in Elmsford hanging around with Armando Capuano, a fellow classmate at Stepinac who planned on becoming an artist when he finished college. Alan and Armando stayed friends long after high school, and even after the Aldas

49

moved back to New York. Armando, in fact, became almost an adopted son to the Aldas and kept in touch with Alan's mother for nearly ten years after the divorce.

When Alan wasn't in Armando's company or busy writing scripts with Joe Colangelo at Stepinac, he was commuting to New Rochelle and the home of the girl he went steady with all through his senior year. "She was with Alan a lot that year," an Elmsford neighbor remembers. "I think she was a student at Good Counsel Academy in White Plains. Alan never introduced her, but she was an awfully pretty thing. Not too tall, I remember. Alan was already approaching six feet and she barely came up to his shoulder."

As overprotective as she might have been in some ways, Joan always made Alan's friends feel welcome when he brought them home, which he did regularly. In fact, Joan was a particular favorite—as far as mothers went—among Alan's classmates at Stepinac. The only time inviting friends home was out of the question was on those afternoons each week when Alan had his piano lesson. It was a refinement Joan had insisted he learn, and she recruited a local teacher named Frank Mando to instruct him at the keyboard.

For all her reclusiveness, Joan left a warm impression on the people in Elmsford who did business with her. "She was a terrific lady, a very, very fine woman," says one storekeeper who still hasn't forgotten her after thirty years. "She was the kind of woman who trusted you completely. She always paid her bills on time and she never bickered about the service. You'd come in and drop a bag of groceries on the table, and she'd have a pile of money waiting on the table. She'd say, 'There, please just take whatever the bill comes to.' She never worried that someone would try and cheat her; she always thought the best of people."

"She was a very high-strung woman," says another old-time resident. "Mrs. Alda was the kind of person who'd flinch if she saw a bee ten yards away. She would panic easily in the face of little emergencies. But she was so polite and so generous and soft-spoken. A very gracious person. She was an excellent mother, too. You could tell she just preferred going about her life up here, raising her son, going to church—she wasn't very impressed with show business even though her husband was a big star. I think she would have been very happy to keep living up here, but things just didn't work out."

6

"I'm not interested in fame. I'm not interested in money. I just want my husband to be healthy and not work too much. In fact, that's all we ever argue about, his overworking and my worrying about it. Even when we argue now, it only lasts five minutes; then we're back like it never happened at all."

The woman who recently uttered those words, with warm and glowing affection, was Mrs. Robert Alda. However, she's not the first Mrs. Robert Alda—she's Flora Marino Alda, the woman he met and fell deeply in love with in Europe before the ink was even dry on his American divorce from Alan's mother Joan.

Bob and Flora had to fight numerous legal obstacles in order to be together. In the American press, Joan tried to paint Flora as a selfish, frivolous woman, eager only to satisfy her own whims, someone to whom the sanctity of marriage meant nothing at all. Yet the twenty-five years since then have proven Joan wrong. Flora has turned out to be a devoted and stabilizing anchor in Bob's life. Eventually she even won Alan's blessing, though his loyalty to his mother made him cool at first. In the mid-1950s when Flora appeared on the scene, Alan was caught painfully in the middle as he watched his father leave one family behind for another.

The separation came shortly after the Aldas had left Elmsford and moved back to New York. In the midst of his career lull and marital discord, Bob decided to put three thousand miles of distance between himself and his problems and search for work in Europe. Arriving overseas, he landed a role in a TV series called *The Major Morgan Stories* that was later released in the United States as *Secret File, U.S.A.* After that, he costarred with Gina Lollobrigida in an Italian-French picture called *Beautiful but Dangerous.*

The film was originally supposed to be called *The Most Beautiful Woman in the World,* but Alda later joked that a more apt title would have been *The Three-Ring Circus.* Alda, an American, played an Italian symphony conductor in the film; Anne Vernon, a French film star, played an Italian; and Vittorio Gassman, a bona fide Italian, was cast as a Russian prince. Only Miss Lollobrigida got to retain her own nationality in the script. She was cast as Italian opera star Lina Cavalieri.

But the casting confusion was mild compared to what actually occurred during filming. Since the movie was scheduled to be dubbed into English, Italian and French—for three different movie markets— the actors were allowed to play their scenes in any language they chose. According to Hollywood columnist Joe Hyams, the set became a veritable Tower of Babel. "In most scenes," Hyams reported in the *New York Herald Tribune,* "Alda read his lines in English to Miss Lollobrigida, who replied in Italian, with Miss Vernon speaking in French and Mr. Gassman in Italian or English depending on his fancy."

Since all the *real* dialogue was going to be added

after filming was finished, there was no sound recording system on the set, and cast and crew were free to talk, laugh, curse or even drop equipment while actors were trying to concentrate on executing crucial scenes. Alda's only memory of that unique moviemaking experience was that most of the time he spent in front of the cameras, he could hear profanity being shouted in six different languages.

But the noise level on the set was only a drop in the bucket. The real sound and fury was the turmoil in Alda's own life—a turmoil that was just beginning.

While recovering from the breakup of his marriage and the exhausting pressure of doing one movie after another, Bob decided to vacation at the Hotel Tea, a small charming establishment on the Via Veneto in Rome. Three months before, a young Italian actress, Flora Marino, physically ill and recovering from some family problems of her own, had booked into the same hotel for an indefinite stay. It was September when she arrived and the cast of *The Barefoot Contessa* had just moved out, so rooms weren't as scarce as they were at the bigger Roman hotels.

Flora stayed at the hotel from the end of September right through Christmas Eve, when she met Bob. "I was waiting for my cab at the entrance to the hotel," she remembers, "when another cab pulled up and out stepped this gorgeous man who looked very familiar to me. At first I couldn't place his face, but then it dawned on me: 'Oh, my God, I know this man!' I'd studied piano for several years and Gershwin was one of my favorite composers. I'd seen *Rhapsody in Blue* seven times. I'd just come back to Rome from the Venice film festival, where I'd met Orson Welles, Humphrey Bogart and John Huston, so I wasn't really awestruck at the sight of Robert Alda."

Bob brushed by her on his way into the hotel, but they didn't give each other more than a casual glance.

Flora went out for the afternoon, and later, when she returned to the hotel, the manager casually mentioned that Robert Alda, the American screen idol, had just checked in, a fact he thought would impress her. But Flora kept her cool. "Maybe that's how I got him," she laughs.

She and Bob didn't actually exchange words until a few days later when they ran into each other at the desk in the lobby. Flora was waiting to make a phone call, and Bob stopped by to pick up his mail and messages. She overheard him ask the manager to introduce them, a bit of unexpected formality that completely shattered her image of brash American screen actors.

"He was really reserved," she recalls, "a very pleasant change from the American men I'd met before that." After the manager introduced them, Bob still didn't rush into any hasty overtures. Whenever he'd run into Flora, he'd continue to say hello very formally, make an idle remark about the weather and inquire solicitously if she was enjoying her stay in Rome—nothing more personal than that.

Slowly but surely, Flora was becoming increasingly enchanted by this reserved older man, so charming and polite, so different in person from the screen heart throb she'd once developed a crush on after seeing *Rhapsody in Blue*. One afternoon Flora and her friends were having tea in the lobby when she spotted Bob at the bar. When Bob looked directly at her, she flushed visibly, so much so that one of her friends immediately exclaimed, "Flora, your face is red and your eyes are shiny. Do you have a fever?"

It turned out that her flush was more than just a case of romantic palpitations. She'd actually caught a virus, and that afternoon her temperature rose to 102 degrees. When Bob heard she was ill, he came to her hotel room to ask if there was anything he could do to help. After she recovered, they finally started dating; and a few months later, Alan—who was spending his junior year in college at the Sorbonne—came to Italy to meet the new woman in his father's life.

"We soon became an inseparable trio," Flora recalls. "Alan spoke French very well, and I was fluent myself, so we had no problem communicating. We became friends rather quickly, perhaps because we weren't that far apart in age. Alan was almost twenty and I was less than ten years older than him. Bob was already forty." So although she'd worried that Bob's grown son might not approve of their romance, Flora soon discovered that her fears were groundless. She and Alan developed a brother-sister kind of rapport, which they maintain to this day, and the three of them had a lot of fun touring Europe together that summer.

In the fall, Alan returned to New York for his last year at Fordham, and sometime afterward (the exact date was never publicized) Bob and Flora were quietly married. Shortly after the marriage, Flora became pregnant, but her pregnancy did not prevent her from traveling with Bob back and forth between Europe and America, accompanying him wherever his work took him. Their son, christened Antony Alda (in honor of Marc Antony) was actually born in the French province of Lyon near the Swiss border.

Bob was thrilled by his brand-new fatherhood, but his joy was somewhat dimmed by the ongoing legal battles with his first wife, Joan. From 1955 to 1958, the bitter war between Alan's parents made headlines in all the New York newspapers—and, for Alan, his years at Fordham were a time when family problems almost threatened to engulf him completely. While his father found a safe exit by physically removing himself to Europe, for Alan the only escape was mental. He delved into books, mainly literature and philosophy, searching among the great writers for a haven—a serenity and quietness—that his once-happy home no longer afforded him.

On November 24, 1955, the *New York Daily News* ran a large photo of his mother, stylishly dressed and bejeweled, looking reminiscent of an innocent June Allyson. But the equally large headline under the photo was far from innocent. It proclaimed: *"Guys and Dolls Guy's Doll Is Being Evicted,"* referring to the fact that nineteen-year-old Alan and his mother were on the verge of being thrown out of their apartment suite at the Hotel Beverly on East 50th Street, because Joan owed $2,500 in back rent. The eviction was supposed to take place on the 24th, but since it was Thanksgiving, the hotel had given her a one-day reprieve.

Apparently, Joan Alda's rent problems stemmed from the fact that she and her estranged husband were unable to come to terms on alimony. Just five months before, she and Alan had been evicted from the family's Sutton Place apartment. In a particularly poignant footnote to that skirmish in the Alda divorce war, the eviction notice had arrived on June 24, her thirty-ninth birthday. On October 27, Joan had filed for a legal separation in Manhattan Supreme Court, and the judge had ordered Alda to pay her $300 a week in temporary alimony until the case actually came to trial. Mrs. Alda, in her trial brief, claimed that her husband's income was in the neighborhood of $100,000 a year, but Alda insisted that the figure was false.

As the weeks wore on, and Alan and his mother were shunted from one temporary residence to another, the cross-accusations between his parents grew more and more embittered.

Joan Alda told the press that her husband had tried to stifle and dominate her during their twenty-three years of marriage, that he forced her to play the role of a clinging vine, totally helpless and dependent on him, so that he could always take stage center. Worse yet, she alleged, he ignored her pleas for financial aid, even when she and her son were being threatened with eviction. "He often warned me," she charged, "that if I took him to court, he would quit work."

Alda, on the other hand (who was unable to return to New York because of screen commitments in Europe), felt that he wasn't being given a fair chance to present his side in court. Was it possible that Joan's well-publicized dramatics were simply her way of punishing her errant husband for deserting her? By appearing homeless (forcibly evicted, in fact) and drawing press attention to her plight, she was certainly hurting Bob's image and career in a very palpable way. Moreover, every new legal battle kept their tortured relationship alive, even if only to spark new outbursts of fury between them.

Alan was hopelessly torn by his love for both his parents. He found himself continually drawn onto the battleground, no matter how hard he tried not to judge either his mother or his father. It would take him a long painful time to understand, and accept, his father's desertion; but eventually he'd realize that neither of his parents was truly wrong or right. If Bob had opted for freedom at the expense of his family, then perhaps Joan's emotionalism and possessiveness had helped to drive him away.

On Joan's birthday, in 1955, when their Sutton Place landlord ordered them to pack their belongings and move, Robert Alda had actually returned to the U.S. to star in a nightclub version of *Guys and Dolls* in Las Vegas. Alan had telephoned his father in Vegas to explain their plight and plead with him to send rent money quickly to bail them out. According to Joan, although Bob had promised Alan that the money was on its way, the check never came. At that time, he was earning $3,000 a week for headlining at the Las Vegas club.

In July 1957, when Robert was already deeply involved with Flora Marino, his American divorce from Joan still wasn't final. In January, she'd won a $900-a-month alimony and separation agreement, but Alda, anxious to speed up the final dissolution of the marriage so that he could wed Flora, had quietly instituted his own divorce proceedings. Joan, now living at 170 Second Avenue in New York, ordered her lawyers to fight that divorce suit, fearful that if Alda won the decree, instead of her, her financial support might be lessened considerably. In New York Supreme Court, she told the judge that her husband, who'd filed suit in Nevada last June, wanted the divorce for only one reason—he planned to marry an Italian movie star "whose tastes are so expensive he won't be able to pay his alimony to me." Without mentioning Flora Marino by name, Joan publicly characterized her as a threat to her own financial and emotional security. "I am informed," Joan proclaimed, "that he and this woman have been publicly cavorting on the continent and they have become the gossip of the international set in Rome and elsewhere." Joan's attorney, Amos S. Basel, challenged Alda's right to file for divorce in Nevada, claiming he was not a permanent resident there. At the time, in fact, Robert was starring with Dorothy Lamour in a summer stock production in Fayetteville, N.Y.

In a statement to the press, Joan announced that Bob was now $1,500 behind in his alimony payments, and she stated: "If he takes on two wives, my support will certainly be affected because he will be required to support a second wife and it will make it even more difficult to support me.

"If he marries the woman he has been courting I

am informed that her tastes are so expensive that I will be in real jeopardy of ever receiving any further money."

Nevertheless, despite all of Joan's attempts to remain Mrs. Robert Alda, on November 20, 1957, a Las Vegas court awarded Bob a final divorce decree ending their twenty-five-year marriage. The basis for the decree was mental cruelty. But even a legal dissolution of the marriage didn't bring about a permanent cease-fire. As late as April 1958, Joan Alda was back in court in New York, claiming that her ex-husband was now $2,500 in arrears in his alimony payments to her.

In the years since, as the anguish between his parents has subsided, Alan has refrained from publicly mentioning the divorce at all. "I love my father," he steadfastly maintains, and Alan, his wife Arlene and their three daughters maintain a warm and friendly relationship with Bob, his wife Flora, and Alan's half brother Antony. Alan rarely mentions his mother in print at all, except to remember her as a very loving and affectionate woman.

But in 1976, in a revealing interview for *Redbook* magazine, he did let his guard down a little with writer Sue Edmiston. "I wouldn't want to talk a lot about my feelings as a child," he confided. "There are still people who could be affected by what I'd say. While there are plenty of positive things that I got from my mother and father, there are some things that had to be worked out, some unresolved feelings I had—that *most* people have toward their parents that we transfer to other people. I think in a way it's *everybody's* lifework to understand the relationship they had with their parents when they were very young, before they could verbalize their feelings."

Undoubtedly, Alan is the product of both Robert Alda and Joan Browne. From his mother came the sensitivity that molded him into a sincere, compassionate human being; from his father, the grit and ambition to survive against occasionally impossible odds in show business. And, ironically enough, from the mistakes his parents made with each other, the determination to guard and nurture his own private life with an intensity rarely seen in Hollywood. If Alan Alda is America's family man *par excellence*, it's simply because he's a child who learned the lessons of pain, as well as the lessons of love, from a failed husband and a defeated wife.

7

By 1957, when his parents were in the final skirmishes of their legal battle, flinging charges and counter-charges that echoed from Las Vegas to New York, Alan was no longer up for territorial grabs in their emotional tug-of-war. He was now a somewhat disinterested spectator, having removed himself both from his mother's home and his father's new family. Alan was busy trying to establish firm foundations for a family of his own. Shortly after his twenty-first birthday, Alan married Arlene Weiss, a graduate of Hunter College and a talented musician.

Their meeting was somewhat subdued for their age and times. It took place not at a noisy college mixer or fraternity party but in a setting that suited both their intellectual tastes. Alan was in his senior year at Fordham, just home from his year abroad at the Sorbonne, when he was invited to a chamber-music concert at a friend's Manhattan apartment. One of the performers was a young clarinetist, Arlene, a Jewish girl from the Bronx, slightly older than Alan's twenty years. Alan found Arlene attractive and easy to be with, but it took him three weeks to get up the nerve to ask her for a date. They spent the evening at the opera, and afterward began seeing each other exclusively.

Following graduation from Fordham, Alan had to fulfill his ROTC commitment by serving six months of active duty in the Army. He was sent to Georgia, where he trained as a gunnery officer, while Arlene accepted a job with the Houston Symphony Orchestra. During their time apart, Alan and Arlene kept up a furious correspondence, counting the weeks, days and hours until they'd be together again.

As Alan saw it, his six-month hitch with Uncle Sam was just an unavoidable delay in achieving the two most important goals in his life—marrying Arlene and establishing himself as an actor. But little did he realize that in a crazy, reverse way his Army training would come in very handy years later on *M*A*S*H*. If Alan hadn't hated Army life so much, he never would have been able to play Hawkeye Pierce so passionately—and so convincingly.

Hawkeye, the first pacifist in uniform ever seen on prime-time television, was truly an extension of Alan himself. His six-month stint as a very apathetic soldier had given Alan a chance to observe military life firsthand; and it had only strengthened the peace-loving attitudes he'd started to develop in college. Later, his unpleasant memories of life as a raw recruit would help him fashion some of his best scripts for *M*A*S*H*.

In 1974, reminiscing with *Good Housekeeping* reporter Joseph N. Bell, Alan recalled with a shudder of disgust his unhappy hitch as a gunnery officer. "I was teaching people how to kill the greatest number of other people with a single mortar round. After every session I'd go home with a terrible knot in my stomach because I was really throwing myself into the job, applying all the talents I had to teaching murder."

Even Alan's sense of patriotism couldn't help him rationalize what he did on the rifle range. He couldn't excuse teaching warfare by the glib argument that a strong defense is the best means of preserving peace. He ultimately came to the very personal conclusion that "I don't think there is a time for war"—and although he faithfully fulfilled his military obligation, he never felt proud of having toted a rifle for his country. Thirteen years later, he only agreed to accept a starring role on *M*A*S*H* after eliciting a promise from the producers that the scripts would never glorify military operations, but would focus instead on the human insanity of the Korean War. All the leading characters on *M*A*S*H* are members of the medical corps, not war strategists or active combat men. They're heroic because they save lives, not because they mutilate and destroy the enemy.

After his Army discharge, Alan headed for Texas, where he and Arlene were married. Without much hesitation, she gave up her concert ambitions so that Alan could concentrate on launching his own career as an actor. At the age of twenty-one, Alan already had a fair measure of semiprofessional experience behind him. At the age of nine and just recovered from polio, he had joined his father onstage at the Hollywood Canteen to entertain World War II GIs; and at Sunday barbecues on the ranch, when many of his dad's friends from Warner Brothers showed up for potluck, Alan would delight them with his original skits. In high school, he had spent almost all his free time under the footlights; and at the age of sixteen he had worked as an apprentice in summer stock. In his senior year at Fordham he had even sandwiched in a brief Broadway debut as Don Murray's understudy in a play that had opened and closed during Alan's midwinter vacation break. In fact, Alan had been able to attend rehearsals, be on call during the out-of-town tryouts, and see the play through its New York birth and death pangs without even missing a single day of college classes.

Four years after Alan and Arlene were married, he returned to Broadway on a slightly more solid footing in Ossie Davis' comedy *Purlie Victorious*. The play, which satirized racial stereotypes in the Deep South, cast Alan in the role of Charlie Cotchopee, a plantation owner's son. His role wasn't large enough for the New York critics to single out his performance, but the play afforded him an opportunity to work with such memorable talents as Ossie Davis, Ruby Dee, Beah Richards and Sorrell Booke. *Purlie Victorious* opened in New York in September 1961 to favorable, if not ecstatic, reviews. It only lasted 261 performances, although Alan later recreated his role in the film version, *Gone Are the Days*.

At that point, the Aldas had spent three years of their marriage in Ohio, where Alan studied acting on a Ford Foundation grant at the Cleveland Playhouse. Back in New York, Alan had done a short-lived off-Broadway comedy, *A Whisper in God's Ear*, and a musical revue called *Darwin's Theories* that he'd co-authored with Darwin Venneri. And, in between those less than lucrative credits, Alan took just about any job he could to support his wife and growing family.

The list of his occupations on his 1960 income tax return covered nearly every possible job category in the *New York Times* want ads. Alan worked as a clown at supermarket and gas-station openings; he was a doorman at the Forum of the Twelve Caesars, a posh New York restaurant; he drove a cab, sold mutual funds, did retouching on baby photographs, and once earned $25 for allowing himself to be hypnotized as part of a psychiatric research experiment.

Selling baby pictures, he recalls, was the financial low point (his income only averaged 12 cents an hour), but working as a supermarket clown proved a definite hazard to his health. Once some preteen delinquents chased him up a street lamp, trying to steal the balloons he was giving out. With the kind of totally antiheroic survival instinct that he'd one day incorporate into the character of Hawkeye Pierce, Alan took a very firm course of action against his pint-sized pursuers: He tossed the balloons to them, climbed down the lamp post, quit the job and went home.

When not climbing down lamp posts, Alan was busy trying to boost himself up the ladder of success. He took all the theatrical assignments he could. On Broadway, he appeared in *Cafe Crown*, a musical, and a pair of comedies, *Fair Game for Lovers* and *Only in America*. Unfortunately, his theatrical reputation didn't escalate much, although his Blue Cross premiums certainly did. According to Alan, most of the Broadway shows he did in the early 1960s had the same tired romantic formula. The bumbling hero he played would break up with his girlfriend and rush off to get roaring drunk—like clockwork—at the end of the second act. The third act would open with Alan lying on a couch, shoes off, suffering from an agonizing hangover. Since Alan had to play that scene in his bare feet, his six-foot-two-and-a-half-inch frame was always getting him into trouble. Stage couches were made for shorter actors, so he was constantly hobbling home from the theater with a stubbed toe. Whenever Alan sprained a toe on the third-act couch, his howls were sure to get a laugh from the audience; unfortunately, the pain he endured playing those scenes was very real.

An even worse encounter came when his clothes accidentally caught on fire one opening night. But instead of panicking, Alan started slapping at his body until the flames died out. The audience applauded wildly, thinking it was an ingenious gag, part of the show, but actually Alan was just trying to save himself from first-degree burns. Luckily, he didn't have to be hospitalized, but he carried the blisters with him for several weeks.

Occasionally, Alan would also land featured one-shot roles on nighttime television. He worked with George C. Scott on an episode of *East Side, West Side*, with Peter Falk on *Trials of O'Brien*, and with Shirl Conway and Zina Bethune on *The Nurses*. But his most memorable video stint came in the fall of 1964 when he joined the cast of *That Was the Week That Was*, a wicked, zany comedy show dedicated to the premise that nothing in America was sacred. *That Was the Week That Was* satirized American politics with a brutal frankness never seen on television before or since.

TW3, as the program quickly became known in show-business shorthand, was done live at the same NBC studio in New York's Rockefeller Center that later would serve as the home of *Saturday Night Live*. The show used comedy sketches, news reports and outrageous songs to make fun of reigning political figures of the 1960s like the Kennedy clan, Lyndon Johnson, Barry Goldwater and Nelson Rockefeller. No one and nothing was safe from the glare of the *TW3* spotlight. One week, a phony news report declared that U.N. paratroopers had just landed in Jackson, Mississippi, to rescue civil-rights workers; the next week, the whole cast introduced a new top-forty hit called "The Vatican Rag." At the time, Vice President Humphrey was under scorching political fire from disenchanted liberals for allowing himself to become Johnson's well-publicized errand boy. So the harried Veep had a special *TW3* musical number written in his honor called "Whatever Became of Hubert?"

During its two freewheeling seasons on NBC, *TW3*

assembled a cast of incredible comedic proportions: David Frost, Elliot Reid, Nancy Ames, Buck Henry, Patricia Englund, Phyllis Newman, Henry Morgan and Bob Dishy. Alan Alda was brought in as a regular during the show's second year to play Patricia Englund's husband in a running domestic skit, written by Bill Brown, future lyricist of *The Wiz*. Like Miss Englund and several other members of the *TW3* troupe, Alan had previously worked with New York's famed *Second City* improvisational troupe which launched such comic rockets as Mike Nichols, Elaine May, Barbara Harris and Alan Arkin.

Patricia Englund vividly remembers her first encounter with Alan Alda, in the early 1960s, when they both were doing improvisational comedy "sets" at Circle in the Square East in New York's Greenwich Village. The fact that Alan was the son of an imposing show-business celebrity needn't have impressed her much, considering Patricia's own family background. Her mother was Mabel Albertson, the perennial wise-cracking matriarch in countless TV sitcoms; her uncle was Jack Albertson; her brother was film and television producer George Englund; and her brother's wife was Cloris Leachman. Patricia herself, though only a few years older than Alan Alda, had been a stage professional since she was a teenager.

At the time she met Alan, he was part of another off-Broadway comedy troupe called *The Premise*, and the whole cast had been invited over to Square East to do a guest stint with *Second City*. "I walked into the theater one day," she recalls, "and somebody said to me, 'That's Robert Alda's son up there.' All I felt, to be perfectly frank, was a slight irritation, because the first thing you sensed about him was this eager-beaver attitude. He had this incredible drive that didn't let up for a second, even in rehearsal. Actually, in retrospect, I realize it wasn't really his problem,

68

but mine. Alan wasn't mean-spirited at all. He was really very ingenuous. It's just that he was so enthusiastic, it was a little upsetting. He tried to be friendly and charming, but I guess I was stand-offish. It was just one of my idiosyncratic things."

Even though they rubbed each other the wrong way at first, later on, when Patricia worked closely with him on *That Was the Week That Was*, her whole impression changed. "I got to be very fond of him," she says, "and grew to have a lot of regard for the kind of human being he was."

In a sense, Alan Alda was almost two different people. On the surface, at rehearsal, Alan was definitely "the group leader," the last one to take a break and the first one back on the stage to wrestle with a difficult scene for the umpteenth time. The other actors in the cast seemed to gravitate naturally around him like satellites, even though he was only a minor member of the cast compared to Buck Henry, Phyllis Newman, Pat Englund and Elliot Reid. His watchword at rehearsal became "Come on gang, let's try it again!" Alan refused to give up until he'd made every moment of a scene come alive. He was constantly ad-libbing and inventing comic bits to strengthen the material that the writers were feeding the performers under fast and grueling deadlines.

But Alan the group leader was only half of Alan the man. As Patricia Englund remembers him, "He wasn't a stuffed shirt or anything like that, just a very uncompromising individual with a strong set of principles. The most amazing thing about him was his intelligence, which came through at quieter moments. Working on *TW3*, we'd have long, tedious hours of rehearsal breaks—either because the writers were still finishing material for us or because union regulations demanded time off for the stagehands—and during those interminable breaks most of the actors would sit around and talk. That's when I noticed that Alan was interested in a whole range of subjects—esoteric, intellectual things—that actors usually couldn't care less about. He'd talk about literature and philosophy and ESP. He was always asking the rest of us, 'What do *you* think about that?'"

That character trait of raising provocative questions—and demanding that they be addressed—was a quality that Alan later gave to Jack Burroughs, his fictional counterpart in *The Four Seasons*. In a recent appearance on *The Phil Donahue Show*, Alan admitted that in fleshing Burroughs out, it dawned on him that his own lifelong penchant for cross-examining other people intellectually was probably a very manipulative trait.

But Patricia Englund thinks Alan was being too hard on himself. "If I'd been on *Donahue*," she says, "I'd have told Alan that's not manipulative at all. I'd have said, 'Why don't you take credit for trying to stimulate a conversation among actors about something else besides what's on page one in *Variety* and who just signed a contract with Joe Papp?' I rather admired that quality about Alan—that he had such a wide spectrum of interests, that he could discuss anything from existentialism to diapering babies. In that sense, he wasn't like an actor at all."

TW3 was done on a tight, two-day rehearsal schedule each week. It kept the energy fresh and the pace fast, but put a tremendous physical and emotional strain on the actors. The show aired live every Tuesday night from 9:30 to 10:00 P.M. (EST) and the writers were literally reworking scripts right up until zero hour. Because nothing was ever poured in concrete until the last possible moment, the actors rarely bothered to memorize their lines. Instead, they usually relied on the teleprompter to bail them out if they "went up" on air. But it wasn't exactly a foolproof safety net. Since lines were rewritten so close to the wire, there was always the danger that the stagehands wouldn't be able to feed the new rewrites into the teleprompter in time for the air show.

In one opener for the show, Buck Henry was supposed to be a national politician and Patricia Englund was interviewing him outside the White House—when they both looked at the teleprompter and visibly froze. It was turned to the wrong page of the script, and there was no way a stagehand could move over to adjust it without actually walking on camera. While the cameraman frantically readjusted his shot so that Buck and Patricia were visible only from the waist up, the stagehand quickly slipped them his scriptbook. With one hand, Patricia held the book somewhere between her knees and the floor, while she and Buck stole glances at their lines and did a fair amount of outrageous ad-libbing in between. What did upwards of thirty million viewers think? "They probably thought Buck Henry was just playing a lecherous politician, trying to look up my dress every time he glanced down at my knees," Patricia laughs.

That kind of mishap was par for the course, actually, in the frantic days of live television. For Alan Alda, this show was perhaps the best education in the world. Every Tuesday night, he was out there alone, with only his own talent, timing and comic instincts to save him from falling on his face. Moreover, *TW3* gave him an invaluable chance to work with some of the brightest and most biting performers in the business.

Aside from the technical difficulties of putting the show together week after week, Alan also learned a great deal about the pitfalls of attempting whacky, scathing satire on mainstream television. Some of the religious, social and political issues that the show courageously tackled were so sensitive that censorship and the threat of lawsuits constantly hung over the producers' heads like a double sword of Damocles. On the whole, NBC tried to give *TW3* a rather free hand creatively, but nevertheless last-minute network and sponsor censorship more than once resulted in the withdrawal of a scene just before airtime. And since people in the news often became the butt of some very stinging routines, the show was insured by Lloyd's of London in case legal problems ensued.

But even Lloyd's got nervous when one of the show's fledgling writers, future feminist champion Gloria Steinem, came up with a particularly touchy gag for one script. *TW3* regularly awarded booby prizes to dubiously distinguished Americans, and Gloria came up with the topper to end all toppers: the Margaret Sanger Award for Family Planning, which she bestowed on a woman (who will herein remain nameless) in Ohio for producing ten children, fifty-two grandchildren, and 185 great-grandchildren. The only trouble was that the woman who received the booby prize was an actual person whose name had been pulled from a recent newspaper obituary. The morning after the fateful show aired, *TW3* was sued by the woman's heirs to the tune of $250,000. NBC and Lloyd's of London were fit to be tied—and the brand of tunafish that sponsored the show nearly flipped its lid—but eventually the court case petered out because of a technicality regarding where the suit was filed.

Gloria Steinem, whose pen prompted this wacky nonsense suit, would later reteam with Alan on a far more serious issue. During the 1970s, when he emerged as an active supporter of the Equal Rights Amendment, Alan and Gloria often shared the podium as they barnstormed the country campaigning for this crucial piece of feminist legislation. But during the time they worked on *TW3*, they didn't really get to know each other. The writers and actors had little contact, and even among the cast there was barely any socializing after the show, since the group spent only two days a week in the rehearsal hall. Alan, moreover, appeared in only one skit per episode, and whatever backstage camaraderie did develop existed mainly among the show's principals. Patricia Englund and Phyllis Newman, for example, often drove home together, since Phyllis and her husband, composer Adolph Greene, were renting a weekend house in Westport, Conn., where Patricia and her family lived.

But Alan did spend a very memorable afternoon with Patricia in 1965—on the day of the Great New York Blackout. Since they portrayed husband and wife on *TW3*, they'd been sent out on a joint casting call for a television commercial. In those days, taped auditions were still a relatively new phenomenon in the advertising business, and the tape machines would break down with exasperating frequency. So that afternoon, when the cameras started going out, Alan and Patricia didn't think anything was amiss. Finally, there was a complete blackout in the building, and for a few frenzied moments the crew actually believed their faulty equipment had blown all the fuses. The rest of the audition was canceled, and Alan and Patricia both walked down the stairs, since none of the elevators seemed to be operating. When they emerged onto Fifth Avenue, they saw a city in total darkness. Patricia instantly decided it was an air-raid attack; but Alan, realizing it was probably a black-out due to electrical overloads in the summer heat, calmed her. Then they both set out separately to walk miles and miles home, since all transportation in Manhattan had come to a halt.

"Whatever you do, don't take the Third Avenue

Bridge," Alan kidded her. The Third Avenue Bridge had become a standing cast joke after Patricia had driven Phyllis Newman home to Connecticut one night and wound up in Harlem instead. At the time, Patricia was on an austerity kick and decided to save the toll by avoiding the Triboro Bridge, her usual route out of Manhattan and into the Bronx. But somehow, searching for the toll-free Third Avenue Bridge, she'd become totally lost in the unfamiliar streets of Harlem for two hours. Meanwhile, her slightly uneasy passenger had grown more and more nervous, especially since this was 1964, the summer of the New York race riots.

Patricia and Phyllis survived the Third Avenue Bridge—and the whole cast made it through the Great Blackout—but *TW3* came to a swift oblivion in 1965. Perhaps it was too controversial to last. After the demise of *That Was the Week That Was*, Alan concentrated his efforts on motion pictures and Broadway, and didn't return to television until three years later. His video reprise came on July 23, 1968, when he made his first of dozens of appearances on the syndicated version of *What's My Line*. Alan, along with Bert Convy, Gene Shalit, Jack Cassidy and Henry Morgan, took turns rounding out the male half of the game panel.

Occasionally, Gene Rayburn was also a guest panelist; and since he and Alan shared the same uninhibited sense of humor, the show dreamed up unique skits for them to delight the home audiences. One mystery guest was a lady house painter who remained steadfastly noncommittal on the subject of brush painting versus roller painting. So the host gave Gene a brush and Alan a roller and let the boys argue it out with two cans of paint in front of an eight-foot wall. After a few minutes, though, Gene got bored with simple wall strokes and decided to paint Alan, who in

74

turn took his roller and smeared Gene's back. Gene then painted Alan's chest, and by the time the show was fading off the air that day, they were both dripping in latex enamel from head to foot—and the argument still hadn't been settled.

Another time, Alan actually won a free bicycle for his daughters on *What's My Line*. The guest who turned out to be his benefactor was a young woman from a company that manufactured burglar alarms for bikes. The mechanism was so delicately built that the alarm would go off at the slightest touch. Alan, however, refused to believe that he could be outwitted by a mechanical gizmo, no matter how ingeniously it had been designed. So, the bet was on: If Alan could confound the bicycle-alarm gadget, he'd get to keep the bike; and either way it would make a wonderful video stunt. The female guest brought the bike on stage, put the kickstand down, and set the alarm. Then, Alan Alda rose to face his two-wheeled nemesis.

In his book *What's My Line? The Inside History of TV's Most Famous Panel Show*, producer Gil Fates recalls: "Rising to the challenge, Alan Alda approached the bike carefully. He circled it, examining the mechanism from every angle. Then he very gingerly picked it up and—without a peep from the alarm—tiptoed it into the wings." The audience cheered wildly at Alan's successful debut as a cat burglar, although the company that made the bike alarms probably wasn't too thrilled by the publicity.

8

All through the 1960s, Alan hopscotched from one medium to another, taking quick stabs at Broadway, motion pictures and television, swinging back and forth like a bewildered mechanical figure on a pendulum. He was still an actor in search of himself, a man without a real sense of direction, and his professional life was as tumultuous as the decade that shaped it. If America at large was caught in a whirlpool of political unrest and rebellion, Alan in particular felt unhinged and without a firm footing of his own. His life in show business was anything but predictable, alternating between dizzying highs and the bleakest lows. In 1963, he repeated his *Purlie Victorious* role for the film version, entitled *Gone Are the Days*, but it was hardly an auspicious screen debut. At a time when the civil-rights protest had become a national powder keg, this mild and humorous view of American race relations failed to catch fire on screen, and *Gone Are the Days* was gone and forgotten by moviegoers all too soon.

A season later, things perked up a bit for Alan when he returned to Broadway in a new comedy called *Fair Game for Lovers*, while simultaneously working on television's *TW3*. Cast as Benny, a laughably lovestruck graduate student, Alan was hailed by critics for his "undiscourageable brightness" in the face of a comedy script lacking only one key ingredient—funny lines. Although the play ran only briefly, Alan's standout performance earned him a far bigger prize before the season was over in *The Owl and the Pussycat*. Cast as Felix Sherman, a frightened and bookish bachelor who befriends a tough black prostitute and then amazes himself by falling in love with her, this bittersweet comedy hit gave Alan his first really substantial stage role. On opening night, he went from simply being Robert Alda's promising young son to a talked-about, written-about, raved-about leading man.

It was the first turning point in Alan's career. But despite the fact that the play enjoyed a healthy Broadway run, even this success held disappointments for him. That spring, when the Tony nominations were announced, Alan's costar Diana Sands found herself entered in the best-actress race, but both Alan and the play were overlooked. Later, his frustration grew even sharper when the play was sold to Hollywood without Alan as part of the screen-version package. After the script was kept on ice in Hollywood for nearly six years, the part of Felix Sherman went to George Segal, who at that time was considered a far more bankable star at the box office. In fact, by the time the film was released in 1970, it bore almost no resemblance to the original Broadway play. The interracial love theme had disappeared completely, and the character of the tough and surly black prostitute magically emerged as the white and almost middle-class Barbra Streisand.

So while *The Owl and the Pussycat* gave Alan a brief taste of triumph, in the end it became merely one more fine but quickly forgotten credit on an already lengthy résumé. Late in 1965, he was still anxious for guest shots on episodic television whenever he could get them, because cops-and-robbers shows helped pay the bills, and after all, any kind of acting work was more satisfying than none at all. As Alan later told *TV Guide*, "I did shows like Peter Falk's *Trials of O'Brien* and was absolutely terrible. But I kept doing them to see if I could lick the problem of jumping into character at a moment's notice." Nevertheless, doing one-shots on other people's TV series wasn't a very comfortable experience. The regulars in the cast were usually a pretty tight group, and transient guest stars like Alan rarely had time to make friends or work into the role before the assignment was up. As Alan succinctly put it, "It was like being a stranger in somebody else's home."

In 1966, Alan was back on Broadway, costarring with Barbara Harris (his old friend from *Second City*) and Larry Blyden in a new musical called *The Apple Tree*. From the beginning, this show promised to be something special. The score was written by Jerry Bock and Sheldon Harnick, the songwriting team responsible for *Fiddler on the Roof*; and Mike Nichols, the new boy wonder of Broadway, was slated to direct it on the heels of his directorial triumphs in *Barefoot in the Park* and *The Odd Couple*. And with material based on the stories of Mark Twain, Frank Stockton and Jules Feiffer, how could *The Apple Tree* miss?

In the three separate one-acts that made up the evening, Alan played Adam in the *Garden of Eden*, a vacillating gladiator in *The Lady and the Tiger*, and Flip—a Casper Milquetoast character who lives a Cinderella fantasy as a rock-'n'-roll superstud—in *Passionella*. In each act, Barbara Harris played another variation on Eve, the eternal temptress, while Larry Blyden alternated as Satan and Fairy Godfather.

Certainly it was an interesting, and rather unusual, premise for a Broadway musical, but the show hardly achieved the smash proportions that such an illustrious gathering of talent would have seemed to ensure. It opened in New York to positive, if not outright glowing, reviews, and was immediately overshadowed by another musical entry that season, Harold Prince's haunting and evocative *Cabaret*. *The Apple Tree* didn't fail on Broadway, but it didn't become a record-breaking megahit either; and the fact that Barbara Harris was soon suffering from physical and nervous exhaustion because of the incredible demands of her role didn't help backstage morale.

Alan finally won a Tony nomination, as best lead actor in a musical. In the race, he was pitted against three other heavyweight contenders: Jack Gilford for *Cabaret*, Robert Preston for *I Do, I Do* and Norman Wisdom for *Walking Happy*. At the gala awards ceremony, staged in New York and broadcast on national television, *Cabaret* swept the field, winning a record number of awards, including best musical. Barbara Harris was cited as best actress in a musical, while Alan, in a close four-way race, lost to veteran Robert Preston.

Award-wise, in a sense, Alan at least had climbed one notch higher. In *The Owl and the Pussycat* his performance had simply helped his leading lady win a nomination. This time he helped her land the medallion itself. Once again, though, Alan found it impossible to translate his stage success into a lucrative motion-picture contract. *The Apple Tree*, after many reports in *Variety* of possible major studio interest, was never turned into a screen musical, with or without Alan Alda and Barbara Harris. Hollywood simply couldn't figure out a way to convert three separate one-act musicals into a workable screenplay; and besides, by the late 1960s, movie musicals were definitely a declining genre anyway. Most studios were afraid to put their money into lavish song-and-dance spectacles after Julie Andrews, Shirley MacLaine and Barbra Streisand all had major box-office disappointments in *Star!*, *Sweet Charity* and *Hello, Dolly*, respectively.

Twice Alan had starred notably on Broadway, yet neither triumph had sent 20th Century–Fox or Paramount screeching to his doorstep, waving million-dollar contracts in his face. Nor did his prospects on the Great White Way look any more hopeful. Alan, like many young American stage actors, found himself slightly out of step as more and more British imports—and British performers—invaded the Broadway theater market. Except for Neil Simon, most American playwrights (especially serious dramatists like Edward Albee and Tennessee Williams) were in decline, while the new Broadway rage was anything with a made-in-England stamp. Critics and patrons alike were infatuated with things like Harold Pinter's *The Homecoming*, Peter Shaffer's *Royal Hunt of the Sun* and Tom Stoppard's *Rosencrantz and Guildenstern Are Dead*. With so many British imports filling up New York theater space, American actors had to scrounge harder than ever for work, and even those American plays that were being produced had an alarmingly high fatality rate.

It was enough to drive any theater star into psychoanalysis (if he was lucky enough to be able to afford it), but Alan had already gone that route a few years earlier at another low ebb in his career. To this day, his short-term involvement with therapy remains a sensitive subject with him, and Alan has never discussed publicly why he sought therapy. Still, it's a safe guess that his continual sense of frustration as an actor was a prime motivation. Recently, when journalist Carey Winfrey tried to broach the subject with him, Alan replied in a rare burst of anger that his reasons for seeking counseling were strictly his own business. To discuss it, he said, "doesn't serve the readers. If they think that I went there because of my compulsion to be involved in ax murders, that's their problem. My private life is my own business. And the fact is, I felt low and I went to somebody who I thought could help and I felt a lot better when I left him."

Of course, what actor doesn't feel shaky and insecure, whether on the brink of stardom or starvation? But in Alan's case, the sense of drifting was particularly acute; his intense devotion to his wife and three daughters gripped him as much as his dedication to his art. For Alan, striving to make his family secure would always go hand in hand with struggling to make his career secure. It would influence his development as an actor no matter how high up the ladder of stardom he eventually climbed.

9

Following *The Apple Tree*, Alan almost made it into prime-time television. Talent scouts from CBS, believing he had tremendous comic potential, tried him out in two pilots for possible new series—*Where's Everett?* and *Higher and Higher*—but neither one actually made it on the air. Nevertheless, Alan remained in Hollywood, trying his hand at film roles. In 1968, United Artists tapped him to portray George Plimpton, the "ordinary guy" who lives out his gridiron fantasies of playing football with the pros, in *Paper Lion*.

The film was based on Plimpton's real-life experiences of roughing it with the Detroit Lions, and Alan, who'd never even held a football in his hands before, took a real beating trying to make himself look believable in the role. Hollywood columnist Sidney Skolsky later wrote, "Alda lists *Paper Lion* as the toughest film he ever made. The Detroit Lions football team gave him a real workover. He carried the bruises around for months to prove it."

Alan refused to let a stuntman take over for him during the action scenes because he wanted the audience to see and feel what it's like when an amateur gets tackled on the field. Weeks before filming began, he spent afternoons in Overpeck Park, in Leonia N.J., tossing the ball around with friends. But after hours of practice, he still looked awkward and clumsy. So the producers, fearing that Alan might seriously injure himself when he actually had to face the Detroit Lions, called in a professional football tutor to give him some survival tips—Tom Kennedy, a quarterback for the New York Giants. During their first lesson, Kennedy knew his work was cut out for him, as he watched Alan running down the field with the ball. Alan's sprinting style reminded him of a frog trying to jump across a pond. Kennedy informed his pupil that he could think of only one great star who used to run like that—Groucho Marx!

When production began on *Paper Lion*, Alan's lack of physical coordination was still evident. John Gordy, one of the Detroit Lions' top players, asked Alan if he'd ever played football as a kid. Trying to kid his way out of a tough situation, Alan retorted, "My mother wouldn't let me, so she had my orthodontist write a note to school saying it was bad for my braces." Gordy and the rest of the team thought Alda's anti-sports humor wasn't very funny, but they were soon giving him points for his willingness to learn and his indefatigable courage in spite of his clumsiness.

Physically, though, that courage took quite a toll. Before *Paper Lion* was finished, Alan's body was covered with lumps and bruises. Several times during shooting, he required emergency medical treatment for contusions; and long after *Paper Lion* was done, he was still regularly applying ice packs to an injured elbow that refused to heal properly. As Alda confided to Sidney Skolsky, "I took a worse beating than George Plimpton had."

One football play alone was a near killer. The

script required Alan to be on the bottom of a pileup with about two thousand pounds of flesh, led by hulking Alex Karras, weighing him down. The scene had to be choreographed with incredible skill and care to make sure Alan wasn't crushed beyond recognition; and the instant the director yelled cut, everyone quickly unpiled to see if Alan was still in one piece—and breathing. Sure enough, there he was lying head up with a huge grin of triumph on his face.

Working with athletes instead of actors proved to be a real education for Alan. Though he didn't exactly become a gridiron enthusiast, he did develop a lasting respect for all his locker-room buddies and their life-style. He later told *TV Guide*, "The pros were special people. They joked a lot. They had a very reckless outlook. Probably because they face danger so much."

In a sense, making *Paper Lion* represented an exhilarating personal triumph, because Alan, having suffered from polio as a child and having grown up such a devout nonparticipant in sports, had faced a grueling physical challenge and proved he was strong enough to handle it. The lumps and bruises he carried around afterward were as satisfying as any awards he'd ever win for other roles. Ironically, though, what hurt a lot more than his aching bones was the public reaction to *Paper Lion*, a film he'd given so much of himself to make. Although Plimpton's story had been a best-selling book, somehow the screen rendition failed to generate much momentum.

Paper Lion, Alan's first major film, premiered in the fall of 1968 and generally failed to dazzle critics. In a year exceptionally notable for sensitive male screen performances—evidenced by Peter O'Toole's *Lion in Winter*, Alan Arkin's *The Heart Is a Lonely Hunter*, Alan Bates' *The Fixer* and Cliff Robertson's *Charley*—Alan's portrayal of a daredevil journalist turned football player seemed lightweight by comparison. In her review for the *Times*, Renata Adler gave the film points for using real football players like Frank Gifford, Alex Karras and John Gordy and for choreographing dazzling and sensational gridiron moves. But she penalized Alan Alda, the star, for being trapped inside the armor of a character who never really came alive on screen. "What doesn't work is the story or the hero," she maintained. "Although Alan Alda is charming as a Harvard boy among a lot of men who are faster, heavier and more solid than he is, it soon becomes apparent that there is no part for him to play . . . at no point is it convincing that this man is a reporter."

Alan's next motion picture, a comedy called *The Extraordinary Seaman* in 1969, turned out to be a dismal failure for M-G-M, as did *The Moonshine War*, a melodramatic epic set in the hard times of the 1930s, a year later. In 1970, Alan also costarred with Marlo Thomas in *Jenny*, an improbable soap opera about a young man who marries a pregnant girl to solve his problems with the draft board. Despite the fact that Marlo was a hot television property, thanks to five years of starring on *That Girl*, her fans didn't flock to the movie theaters to see her. *Jenny* did only slightly better at the box office than *The Extraordinary Seaman* or *The Moonshine War*.

Film critic Rex Reed raked *Jenny* over the coals as one of the most disappointing releases of 1970, summing up his reaction to it as "big deal." In a particularly scathing review, he wrote: "Marlo Thomas takes out her breasts, folks, and suckles a baby on the screen right before your very eyes. She can't do *that* on TV. Otherwise, *Jenny* might just as well be another weekly installment of *That Girl*."

He found the marriage-of-convenience plot—about a middle-class girl from Connecticut who hooks up with an itinerant young filmmaker in Central Park because she needs a husband for her baby's birth certificate and he needs a Catch-22 for his draft board, about as wholesome and appealing as "a plateful of rattlesnakes."

Furthermore, Rex Reed judged the love story "pitiful" and the characters "silly," but was far more sympathetic in his review of Alan Alda as an emerging comic talent. "What little humor I found in it," Reed wrote, "came not from the script or direction . . . but from the improvisational acting technique of Alan Alda, who looks and talks like Henry Aldrich on speed."

In 1971, Twentieth Century–Fox tried Alan in a different kind of cinematic pose, this time in a supernatural thriller called *The Mephisto Waltz*. Again the box-office response was only lukewarm, and for Alan the most memorable part of that film stint was a pair of bandaged knees, a souvenir from an on-set mishap. During filming, he fell down an entire flight of stairs, smashing his knees into the iron posts at the bottom of the steps. Even two years later, he still complained of severe aches in his knees, as a result of nerve damage.

He was accumulating film credits (and bruises!) and working steadily, but the material he was given to play remained generally mediocre. Alan, it seemed, was caught in the vicious circle that stymies so many Hollywood actors. To become famous, you need to be showcased in outstanding parts, but to get those parts you need to be famous first. Ultimately, it was television, the medium he was least experienced in, that gave him his long-awaited breakthrough role. In 1971, Alan joined an all-star cast including Vic Morrow, Billy Dee Williams and Dean Jagger in *The Glass House*, a made-for-television movie about the grizzly realities of American prison life. Based on a story by

Truman Capote, *The Glass House* was actually filmed on location, behind bars at Utah State Prison, with Alan featured as a college professor convicted of manslaughter.

To this day, Alan still considers it the most artistically satisfying role of his career. The film aired on the *CBS Friday Night Movie* on February 4, 1972—just five months after the Attica prison riots had sent a shock wave through America—and won acclaim for its bold and realistic depiction of convict brutality. Alan's outstanding performance finally gave him the visibility as an actor that he'd waited fourteen years to achieve, although making *The Glass House* hadn't been the most pleasant experience of his career.

If getting mauled in *Paper Lion* and falling downstairs in *Mephisto Waltz* had been harrowing, suddenly that all seemed like child's play compared to the working conditions on this film. On location, the cast was surrounded by real prison inmates, some of whom were serving sentences for violent crimes—and the recent bloody takeover at Attica was still fresh in everyone's mind. In fact, Alan and the rest of the crew were getting ready to leave Utah State Prison when two convicts tackled him, holding a razor to his throat. They announced that they were staging a breakout with Alda as their hostage.

The entire episode lasted only a minute or two, while poor Alan visibly aged several years. It turned out that the whole business was actually a gag perpetrated by Tom Gries, the director of the film, and a pair of friendly, willing inmates. The cast and convicts broke into applause and laughs, but Alan remained badly shaken. It was obvious he didn't appreciate being chosen as the victim in this little caper. His captors might have been harmless, but their razor certainly wasn't, and Alda later sarcastically referred to Gries as a "nice, fun-loving guy."

By 1972, Alan had appeared prominently in six motion pictures and nearly as many Broadway plays. Aside from *The Glass House*, his one and only standout dramatic role, his television career was somewhat limited. And yet in a few months' time, the whole balance would shift. It all started one day during a rehearsal break on *The Glass House*. Alan sat down to read a new script that his agent had just sent him and got so wrapped up in the pages in front of him that he was almost late for his next call on the set.

The script was the pilot for a new CBS comedy series called *M*A*S*H*.

10

In the fall of 1972, the Watergate break-in was still backpage news and Richard Nixon, serenely oblivious to the political timebomb that was ticking away for him, relaxed as he headed toward a landslide reelection as President.

Ironically, that season American television was veering toward a Watergate of its own. While things appeared calm and unchangeable on the surface, new trends in programming were coming to a slow boil, and the magical multimillion-dollar world of prime-time TV would never be the same. A generation of kids who'd been raised on *Bonanza* and *I Love Lucy* were emerging as the new adult viewing audience. These kids had lived through the rebellion of the 1960s, the fall of the Kennedys, the disappointment of Lyndon Johnson's Great Society, and finally the debacle of Vietnam. Sponsors would have to offer something slightly gutsier than slapstick and shoot-'em-up shows to keep these kids hooked. New viewers were demanding more realism from the tired old tube—and risk-takers like producers Norman Lear and Grant Tinker were rushing in to offer it.

Although old-style comedies like *The Doris Day Show* and *The Brady Bunch* continued to ride high in the ratings, a few relatively new sitcoms were striving to be more experimental. *All in the Family*—an unpublicized midseason replacement on CBS—dared to poke fun at bigots, religion and bluecollar America, and succeeded. *The Mary Tyler Moore Show*, another surprise hit, broke ground too, by making a palatable heroine out of a single thirty-year-old career woman with no imminent plans to marry, but no plans to spend every night of her life alone, either.

It was a time of transition—and sheer terror—in prime-time programming, because by 1972 the old success formulas were drying up but nobody had quite figured out what the new formulas should or shouldn't be.

Producer Norman Lear seemed to have the jump on everyone else. On the heels of *All in the Family*, he quickly put together *Sanford & Son*, TV's first truly black sitcom, the story of an irascible junk dealer and his well-meaning son. Then, in the fall of 1972, Lear launched his third weekly comedy by casting Broadway actress Bea Arthur as *Maude*, an outspoken suburban liberal whose heart was always a little bit to the right of her principles.

That same season, MTM Enterprises, owned by Mary Tyler Moore's husband Grant Tinker, introduced *The Bob Newhart Show*, in the same thoughtful mold as Mary's show. This time the setting was a Chicago psychologist's office instead of a Minneapolis newsroom, and the comic foils were Bob Hartley's group-therapy patients instead of Mary Richard's six-o'clock-news colleagues.

That year it seemed as if everyone in prime time was trying their darnedest to be hard-hitting and relevant, down to the last private detail. Each episode of *The Bob Newhart Show* was sure to include an obligatory goodnight scene, with Bob and his TV wife, Suzanne Pleshette, snuggled cozily in their king-sized bed. Meanwhile, week after week, viewers anguished with Maude Findlay over her divorced daughter's sexual liaisons, and her husband Walter's midlife crisis (and nervous breakdown), while Maude herself seemed in a perpetual state of menopausal hot-flashes.

The network where all this was taking place was CBS; and sometimes program planners, in their haste to manufacture sensational ratings, went too far. Perhaps one of the most forgettable new shows of 1972 was *Anna and the King*. Basically, this was nothing more than a rehash of *The King and I*, minus the music, but with a few socially conscious themes snuck in. Another was a new program called *Bridget Loves Bernie*, a romantic farce about an Irish blueblood's daughter and a Jewish delicatessen owner's son. Their main obstacle to happiness seemed to be that Bridget preferred her corned beef with cabbage, while Bernie liked his on pumpernickel or rye. The humor was so embarrassing that the show was eventually removed from the air after heated protests from Catholic and Jewish groups.

And then there was *M*A*S*H*. Relevant, compassionate, smartalecky and wickedly, wickedly funny—a unique television comedy that was set in the early 1950s but seemed as contemporary as anything happening in the news. Based on Robert Altman's 1970 Oscar-nominated movie, *M*A*S*H* focused on the insanity of the Korean War, but drove home a strong point about the horror and hopelessness of war in general. When it first aired on September 17, 1972, United States troops were still engaged in combat in Vietnam—the most unpopular military effort in American history—and festering antiwar sentiment helped give the show instant appeal.

M*A*S*H wasn't the first TV sitcom to poke fun at

the Army, but it took an entirely different tack than any of its video predecessors did. *Sgt. Bilko*, a big hit of the 1950s, had shown officers and enlisted men as bureaucratic goof-offs, but that was very harmless satire, since Bilko's platoon, serving out their hitch in peacetime, might as well have been spending the summer at Boy Scout camp. The only action they saw was a never-ending poker game in their Kansas barracks.

Hogan's Heroes, another humor-in-uniform comedy of the mid-1960s, was actually set behind German lines in World War II, but the viewpoint was totally slapstick. The American POWs turned their stalag into something resembling a college frat house, and their Nazi captors were about as menacing as the Katzenjammer Kids. Before *M*A*S*H* had the courage to deal realistically with the subject, TV combat comedies were a very bloodless, gutless affair. With shows like *Hogan's Heroes* as their only reference point, American kids could actually grow up believing that war is swell.

Despite the show's pacifist outlook, the major characters of *M*A*S*H* were far more heroic than previous generations of video GI's. They weren't con men like Bilko's boys or clumsy oafs like *McHale's Navy*, but doctors and nurses dedicated to saving lives, working in substandard conditions near the battlefront, performing round-the-clock surgery as helicopter units rushed the wounded to their makeshift hospital. In *The Complete Directory to Primetime Network TV Shows 1946–Present*, Tim Brooks and Earle Marsh summarize the basic theme of the show that accounts for so much of its success: "The cast of characters in *M*A*S*H* were all members of the 4077th Mobile Army Surgical Hospital, stationed behind the lines during the Korean War. Their job was to treat the wounded being sent to them from the front lines and to try to save as many lives as possible. The environment was depressing; many of the doctors (who had all been drafted) could not really believe they were living under the conditions to which they were being subjected. There was an overwhelming sense of the futility and insanity of war that permeated their daily lives."

"Suicide Is Painless" was the title of the *M*A*S*H* theme song, and it set the tone for the black humor that haunted every episode. Scenes cut back and forth between critically wounded GI's and the doctors and nurses who treated them, to the off-duty shenanigans that became the hospital personnel's only relief from the holocaust around them. Each character on *M*A*S*H* had his own set of foibles, his own private escape route from the horror he lived with in Korea. Hawkeye Pierce and Trapper John McIntyre kept up an endless round of nurse-chasing, drinking themselves into a stupor, breaking regulations and playing spiteful tricks on their arch-antagonist, Major Frank Burns. Corporal Radar O'Reilly, a shy raw recruit, carried around a teddy bear as a security blanket. Corporal Maxwell Klinger smoked cigars and wore flamboyant women's clothes in his hopeless quest to be declared insane and receive an honorable discharge from the Army. Hot Lips Houlihan, the head nurse, behaved on duty like a female version of Patton, a starched-white martinet totally devoid of human emotion. Then she invited Major Burns into her tent after lights-out at night.

On the movie screen, Donald Sutherland had played Hawkeye, with Elliott Gould as his sidekick Trapper John. Now Alan Alda and Wayne Rogers took over the roles for the television series, obviously hoping that the prime-time edition of *M*A*S*H* would provide them with the same kind of springboards for stardom. For its debut, *M*A*S*H* was positioned on the CBS Sunday night comedy line-up at 8:00 P.M., pitted against two long-running blockbusters—*The FBI* on ABC and *The Wonderful World of Disney* on NBC. It wasn't an ideal launching pad for a new series, but CBS was relying heavily on the smash success of the movie to generate viewer interest.

Alan, however, had some private doubts that ran much deeper than simple concern about an unfavorable time slot. When he first read the script while working on *The Glass House*, he was excited by the freshness of the humor, by the sharp, brittle strokes of humanity that shaped all the characters. Alan phoned his agent immediately, telling him it was the best comedy pilot he'd ever read. But later, as the weeks went by and he drew closer to finalizing a contract, his faith in the project began to waver. Alan worried that if the show became a hit, the originality might be lost after the first few episodes and the quality of the scripts would start to deteriorate. He didn't want to wind up playing a Korean War imitation of Gomer Pyle. He felt the antiwar theme—the message of compassion in combat that made *M*A*S*H* special—had to be protected from network interference at all costs. Otherwise, he dreaded getting tied up with the show on a long-term basis. Alan later told *New York Times* reporter Robert Berkvist, "I wanted to be sure from the start that it wasn't going to turn into one of those hijinks-at-the-battlefront routines."

One night, just before production began, Alan met with Gene Reynolds and Larry Gelbart, the producers of the series, at the Beverly Hills Hotel coffee shop to hash things out. He demanded a firm assurance that the antiwar focus of the show wouldn't be lost as pressure from network and sponsors inevitably grew "to forget the message—just go for laughs."

The producers sat for hours in the coffee shop that

night, listening to Alan's suspicions about the quality of prime-time television. Alan was blunt and unyielding—unexpectedly blunt, perhaps, since everyone in the room knew that he had a lot more to lose than to gain. He might very well be jeopardizing the best career offer he'd had in years. But the problem was that Alan's personal philosophy was at stake. If it were simply a question of billing or salary or the size of his dressing trailer, a compromise might have been reached in minutes. But on an issue of conscience he simply refused to budge. His six-month stint in the Army had left him permanently outraged at the glorification of the military world. Talented as he was, there was simply no way Alan could bring himself to play a character who found war a rowdy, laughable affair.

There was no way Reynolds and Gelbart could skirt the issue. Alan demanded assurances that *M*A*S*H* would actually focus on the brutal side of war rather than simply paint a Walt Disney picture of the battlefront. If the producers had any thoughts of watering the show down to make it more palatable to mainstream America and the sponsors, then he preferred to drop out.

As Alan later said, "I didn't want to be involved in *M*A*S*H* if we were going to take a neutral position on the war. The trouble with war comedies in the past was that they were written as if the characters led some magical, country-club existence in the middle of the battlefront—safe and protected from the horror just outside their bunks."

He knew that television traditionally had an ostrich-like way of avoiding risky, controversial issues. His friend Marlo Thomas, whom he'd recently costarred with in *Jenny*, had spent five years fighting tooth and nail for every inch of ground she broke on her TV series *That Girl*. When Marlo first brought ABC the idea for her own series, her intention was to explore the problems of a feisty, free-spirited single girl, trying to cope with independence. In the end, she wound up playing a lovable scatterbrain, a child-woman totally dependent on her clever boyfriend whenever a crisis arose. Instead of Miss Independence—Marlo's original title for the series—*That Girl* was diluted into an updated version of "Honeybunch Grows Up."

Such were the realities of prime-time television programming even in 1972—so Alan had good cause to beg, plead and bully for quality control in negotiating his first *M*A*S*H* contract. But the producers had good cause to be worried, too. Alan didn't know it at the time, but he was their first and only choice to play ,Hawkeye Pierce. They sensed that his likable image would be a big plus, that his unique gift of blending comedy and poignancy would make him a prime asset in selling *M*A*S*H* to the American viewing public. Therefore, they were willing to bend farther to meet his demands than Hollywood producers are generally known to do to accommodate television actors with an untested Nielsen potential. Furthermore, they were basically in agreement with Alan about the importance of keeping the film's antiwar theme in its move to the small screen. If *All in the Family* could insert sound effects like Archie Bunker flushing a toilet and bypass network censorship regularly, then maybe *M*A*S*H* could get away with inserting clips of helicopters transporting wounded soldiers and surgical scenes where Army doctors battled their own fatigue, plus equipment and supply shortages, in an often futile effort to save lives.

At 2:00 A.M. that night, Alan and his new producers emerged from their summit meeting a little weary, but a lot more hopeful. In the end, Alan had won the assurances that were so crucial to him; and just eight hours later he reported to Twentieth Century–Fox studios to begin rehearsals for the first episode of *M*A*S*H*.

Undoubtedly, the mood of protest against the Vietnam War helped establish the show during its first months on the air. But Alan himself was irritated by newspaper critics who tried to promote the idea that *M*A*S*H* was a cleverly camouflaged political advertisement created and acted by Hollywood liberals hammering home their own viewpoint. True, there was one obvious parallel between Vietnam and Korea—the geographical setting—but Alan felt the similarity was being blown all out of proportion. He wanted his character, Hawkeye, to be viewed as a humanist, not a political missionary. He hoped America would realize that the show's message was an indictment of all war, not just of the struggle in Indochina. It was a message, he felt, that applied just as easily to the fighting in Belfast or the Sinai Peninsula or South Africa.

"The show's bias," Alan explained to Robert Berkvist, "is that *people count*. That may be a kind of greeting-card way of putting it, but it's nonetheless true. We joke a lot, and clown around with the nurses like Hot Lips Houlihan, but we also show the audience that people are getting hurt, mangled and killed."

From the beginning, Alan stepped into the character easily, and they synchronized to a tee. He had no trouble reading Hawkeye's mind, believing his thoughts, tapping the sensitivity that lay under the rough edges of Pierce's comic pose. It was the most exciting—and satisfying—challenge of Alan's career, a role he was truly born to play. Alan and Hawkeye shared a bond of conscience, as humanists, as intellects, as men dedicated to their work. When Hawkeye poked fun at the injustices of the world—some of them big, some of them little—it eased the rage that Alan himself carried deep inside.

Alan understood instinctively what made Hawkeye tick, and he could identify with the M*A*S*H captain's frustrations, too. Here was a talented young surgeon, with a tremendous passion for living, who felt trapped by circumstances beyond his control. The Korean War had interrupted his life and condemned him to an indefinite, horrifying limbo. He was stuck in a primitive hellhole, surrounded by death and destruction, with no hope of escape, repelled by the mad forces of war, yet dependent upon them too, to someday bring about the fragile peace that would be his only chance of release. Although Alan himself had never fought on a battlefront or been forced to endure a semi-civilized existence thousands of miles from home, he arrived on the set of M*A*S*H with fifteen years of another kind of frustration behind him that helped create the darker side of Hawkeye's character. As a struggling actor, Alan had been trapped in his own private limbo for so long that he had no trouble imagining Hawkeye's feelings of isolation and discontent.

What Alan had to create artificially in preparing for the role were some of the broader character traits— the drunkenness and constant womanizing that made Captain Pierce such a lovable scoundrel. Hawkeye the hell-raiser was a very different breed from Alan Alda, the diligent hard-working husband from Leonia, New Jersey. For Alan, this was the pure fantasy part of the role, and he accepted the challenge as simply another step in his actor's education. He launched into it with the same vigor with which he'd plunged into gyrating like a rock singer in *The Apple Tree* or learning to throw a football in *Paper Lion*. And Alan's portrayal of Hawkeye the Nurse Chaser worked beautifully on screen.

Ironically, although Alan never had the rugged looks or rakish charm of a romantic leading man, a great deal of his career had brought him roles where "the mating game" was a dominant theme. As Felix in *The Owl and the Pussycat*, he became an introvert poignantly seduced by a prostitute; as Adam in *The Apple Tree*, he found himself sexually on the defensive once again, as Eve tried to worm her way into his innocent and self-sufficient bachelor cave.

Now in *M*A*S*H*, Alan got to explore the other side of the mating game. Now he was a skirt-chaser, the sophisticated master of the one-night stand. In script after script, Hawkeye wisecracked his way into the hearts (and tents) of willing nurses, only to leave them weeping into their powdered eggs at mess call the next morning. Hawkeye's resistance to marriage and faithfulness—his steadfast credo that the state of love is a temporary aberration of a gullible mind—is the one attitude that truly sets him apart from Alan, his alter ego. After ten years of playing the role, Alan still says he hasn't quite figured out Hawkeye's quirk—why he runs away from a lasting relationship quicker than he'd duck a flying hand grenade from the North Koreans. But it's Hawkeye's sexual single-mindedness, his perpetual backing off from a real commitment to a woman, that most fascinates Alan the married man.

Two or three times during the course of the show, scripts have shown Hawkeye verging awfully close to falling in love, then retreating into his confirmed bachelorhole like a scared jack rabbit. "Love is a feeling that washes over him like a bad cold," Alan says, "and he shakes it off as fast as he can." Hawkeye's inability to give of himself emotionally—to share his life with a woman—may be just another crippling side effect of war. A surgeon who spends day after day dealing with the human rubbles of war, desperately trying to patch up maimed and mutilated bodies and somehow make them whole again, quickly loses faith in the power of love. Perhaps he's witnessed too much dying to believe that a simple, fragile bond between a man and a woman can ease the pain of the world. Physically and emotionally, he pours out so much of himself to the wounded and the dying that he emerges from the operating room morbidly drained. He has nothing left to give another human being on an intimate level, except a few minutes of sexual pleasure to wipe out the horror that surrounds them both.

Fortunately, for Alan, Hawkeye never remained a static character; over the years as he grew and changed, his evolution as a human being helped keep audiences intrigued by him and helped keep Alan's creative enthusiasm flowing. At the start, Hawkeye was much more of a rebel than he is now, constantly baiting his military superiors and pulling outrageous gags on the Army brass that would bring him to the brink of court-martial. As his patience and tolerance grew, his appetite for drinking seemed to decline and now he's rarely seen with a hangover in the scripts. Alan once described Hawkeye's barroom bravado as "a creepy attitude" for a TV hero to have, and it was undoubtedly the one flaw in the character that Alan personally felt most uncomfortable portraying. Knowing that impressionable viewers were watching the show—especially teenagers—Alan didn't like the idea of glamorizing drunkenness as a noble indulgence. Over the years, as his backstage clout grew and he assumed more and more creative control of the show, the liquor laughs got toned down, while new dimensions of maturity were added to Hawkeye's character.

Two years ago, in an interview with movie critic Gene Siskel, Alan noted other differences between himself and the character—significantly, that Hawkeye's a ladies' man, while he's not; also, Alan speaks French fluently and Hawkeye doesn't. He has a much lower cultural threshold. He couldn't care less about classical music, philosophy or poetry. Hawkeye would play Frank Sinatra records if he gave a party; Alan holds chamber-music concerts in his house.

Actually, Alan sees their strongest link as mutual cowardice. "I think we're equally non-brave," he told Gene Siskel, recalling that at times he's run down the streets of New York chasing muggers wondering how in the world he'd actually overpower them if his furiously shaking knees ever caught up with them. Hawkeye—who'd probably try to entertain his way out of a confrontation with the North Koreans by doing a Groucho Marx routine—would probably have the same reaction. "In general," Alan told Siskel, "my attitude—and I suspect, Hawkeye's—is pretty much what Jack Kennedy said when he was asked, 'How did you become a war hero?' And he said, 'It was involuntary. They sank my boat.'"

From the start, however, Alan was no cowardly lion on or off the set when it came to bucking the network brass—and fighting for his own preeminence in the show.

The time-slot war, for example, was a major clash that marked the show's early days. Alan was very vocal in siding with the producers in their bid to get *M*A*S*H* a better viewing time. In its first season on the air, *M*A*S*H* aired on Sunday night, sandwiched between *Anna and the King* and *The Sandy Duncan Show,* two sitcoms that proved to be very short-lived. The last show in that two-hour comedy block was *The New Dick Van Dyke Show,* another disappointing entry. All three programs represented a totally different kind of comedy style from the hard-hitting black humor of *M*A*S*H*. They might have been called pablum dramas, while *M*A*S*H* was problem drama. Created as routine formula comedies, perfect for the whole family to view, *Anna and the King* might easily have been called *Nanny and the Professor Go to Bangkok*; Sandy Duncan was a cute young single girl living in the proverbial cute apartment complex with a pair of stupid, lovable neighbors and a string of stupid, lovable boyfriends; while Dick Van Dyke—now cast as a TV talk host in Arizona instead of a TV comedy writer in New Rochelle—still did the same old pratfalls in his tastefully furnished living room that he'd done for five years on the old *Dick Van Dyke Show*.

Lumped into a programming setup like that, *M*A*S*H* had trouble finding the right audience to attract. So, the next season, in 1973, producers Reynolds and Gelbart fought—and won—their battle to be positioned on CBS next to the network's more daring and provocative comedy series. In the fall of 1973, *M*A*S*H* was switched to Saturday nights, following right after *All in the Family*, now the established number-one show in the weekly Nielsen ratings. At 9:00 P.M., after *M*A*S*H* finished, *The Mary Tyler Moore Show* came on, followed by Bob Newhart and then Carol Burnett. This three-hour block of uninterrupted "thoughtful pandemonium" became one of the most successful programming setups in television history. Most significantly, it helped *M*A*S*H* emerge from low-rated oblivion during its second season. If someone hadn't realized that *M*A*S*H* would draw the same kind of audience as *All in the Family* and *Mary Tyler Moore*, the show might never have survived.

But the switch from Sunday to Saturday night made all the difference in the world. In 1972, when the final Nielsen tallies were computed for the year, *M*A*S*H* didn't even qualify as one of the twenty most-watched programs on prime-time television. In

1973, the picture changed radically. It finished as the fourth most popular program of the year with an audience count just behind *All in the Family*, *The Waltons* and *Sanford and Son*. A year later—even though *M*A*S*H* had now been moved to Tuesday nights to make way for Paul Sands' *Friends and Lovers* on Saturday night—it still ranked fifth for the year. This, in network terms, was perhaps the most significant victory yet. *M*A*S*H* had proved something big. It could sustain an audience no matter where it appeared on the TV schedule. Programmers consider this the mark of a "true hit," a show that can remain a Nielsen leader no matter what night or what time it airs. In any decade, only a few programs ever reach the cherished golden status of a true hit. *M*A*S*H*, in the 1970s, was one of the chosen few. Alan Alda and his wacky cohorts had slowly but surely taken hold of the American public, changing the style of television comedy forever; and at the age of thirty-eight, Alan was suddenly, surprisingly, beginning to think of himself as a star.

By 1975, with ratings in a blockbuster holding pattern and Emmy accolades regularly pouring in, *M*A*S*H* was a firmly entrenched viewing habit. But at the same time, a surprising shift in the focus of the show was taking place. Although Loretta Swit, Larry Linville, Wayne Rogers and McLean Stevenson were all part of the backbone upon which the scripts had been fleshed out for three successful seasons, more and more it seemed that Alan Alda was emerging as the show's premiere talent.

When *M*A*S*H* began, Alan had shared prominence with Wayne Rogers, and the characters of Hawkeye and Trapper John were a tightly interlocking team, continually reacting to each other and sharing center stage. It was impossible to single out either actor as the major star of the show, just as you couldn't separate Penny Marshall from Cindy Williams on *Laverne & Shirley*, or Burns from Allen or Starsky from Hutch. But as Alan's creative control intensified and he began involving himself with writing and directing episodes of *M*A*S*H* as well as acting in them, Wayne Rogers started to feel that his own position was severely threatened. He left the show in a heated contract dispute at the close of the 1974-75 season, a year after Alan won a double set of Emmies as best lead actor in a comedy series and outstanding actor of the year.

With Wayne Rogers' departure, Gelbart and Reynolds chose not to recast the part, but phased out the role completely. In the story, Trapper John McIntyre won his Army discharge and was sent home to the States, leaving Hot Lips and the rest of the 4077th gang to continue grappling with shellshocked soldiers and mentally deficient Army bureaucrats. Wayne's character, however, returned to the screen in 1979 in a far more sober and serious guise—the central figure in a new dramatic series, *Trapper John, M.D.* But it was Pernell Roberts, not Wayne Rogers, who picked up the pieces of Trapper's life, twenty-five years after the Korean War, as the obstreperous head of surgery in a San Francisco hospital. That same season, though, Wayne resurfaced on CBS in another new hit, a comedy called *House Calls*. Ironically, his character of a glib and charming doctor who spent most of his time on duty chasing Lynn Redgrave up and down hospital corridors was much closer to the original Trapper John on *M*A*S*H* than to the middle-aged authority figure in the Pernell Roberts incarnation.

At the point when Wayne Rogers left *M*A*S*H*, Trapper John had shrunk considerably from a captivating antihero into a two-dimensional foil for Hawkeye's antics. Therefore, the show made no effort to find a star of equal stature to create a new sidekick for Alan Alda. The character they did create, Captain B.J. Hunnicutt, was a rather mild sparring partner, compared to his hell-raising predecessor. To play the role of B.J., Mike Farrell, a virtually unknown actor—who'd appeared on the NBC soap opera *Days of Our Lives* in the late 1960s—was hired. Farrell, as Hunnicutt, was likable and soft-spoken. The scripts fleshed him out as a devoted family man who deeply resented the fact that the Korean War had separated him from his wife and daughter. His flagrant fidelity while isolated from his family with no hope of returning to them in the near future was a stark contrast to Hawkeye's live-for-the-moment response to despair. In a strange way, Hunnicutt—the good family man whose foundations could never be shaken—was almost a mouthpiece for Alan Alda's personal beliefs. Since domestic virtue could never be incorporated into Hawkeye's iconoclastic personality, a new character had been invented to promote things that Alda espoused.

At that same time that Wayne Rogers parted company with *M*A*S*H*, McLean Stevenson, who played Lieutenant Colonel Henry Blake, the medical unit's blundering commander, gave notice too. Stevenson was in the process of negotiating a long-term contract with NBC—to develop him as a comedy star in his own right—and felt that three seasons of *M*A*S*H* had given him enough visibility on the tube to make his move. In this case, the writers turned the loss of an actor into one of the show's most poignantly dramatic episodes. For once, the comedy stopped totally as news came that Blake had been killed in a helicopter crash. His successor as post commander was Colonel Sherman Potter, a Regular Army officer as well as a surgeon. Veteran character actor Harry Morgan—whose credits included *December*

Bride, Dragnet, Pete & Gladys and *The D.A.*—was enlisted to portray the starchy but kindhearted Potter,
and a new dimension was added to M*A*S*H. Potter
drove home the point that a career Army man, with
all the spit and polish of Dwight Eisenhower, had an
innate humanity at heart, too. His character became a
bridge of sanity between the bureaucratic higher-ups
and the rebellious doctors. He was just as tired of the
war as Hawkeye and Klinger, but would stick to the
letter of the rules no matter how long the insanity
dragged on.

The departures of Wayne Rogers and McLean Stevenson solidified Alan's position as the show's un-
questioned leading man. Reports of Alan's behind-
the-scenes dominance began to filter out of the
M*A*S*H video compound at Twentieth Century-
Fox. It was well known, for example, that Alan's
relationship with Jackie Cooper, one of the show's
early directors, had been far from amicable. Again,
Cooper left M*A*S*H, while Alan stayed—more secure than ever—adding fuel to the fiery and persistent
rumors of Alda the power grabber. Some insiders asserted that Alan, personally, had difficulty coexisting
with other strong male egos on the set, and that he
was much more compatible working with women.
Loretta Swit, who played Hot Lips Houlihan—the
only female regular in the cast—was known for being
irritable and abrasive during rehearsal. Yet Alan's attitude remained patient and forgiving, or at least
never led to the kind of head-on confrontation that
made her not renew her contract.

His relationship with Larry Linville, who played
Major Burns, was apparently less cordial. Linville
stayed with the series for five seasons, then followed
Wayne Rogers and McLean Stevenson's lead and
quit. Actress Vana Tribbey, who was married to Linville during the last two years of his stint on

M*A*S*H, refused to discuss Alda when approached by this biographer. She cringed visibly, mentioning only that her ex-husband's dealings with Alan—on a business level, as she put it—were exasperating, although she agreed that personally Alan was as charming and considerate as his reputation in newspapers and magazines would have you believe.

Burns, the whimpering and duplistic archvillain of the series, had been the show's resident "Ted Baxter" for six years, and a new whipping boy was needed to give Hawkeye and Huniccutt an available butt for their weekly gags. Again, rather than recasting the role, Burns was transferred to another unit after his longtime mistress Hot Lips married Colonel Donald Penobscott. Since that left the 4077th one surgeon short, Major Charles Emerson Winchester—stuffed-shirt Ivy Leaguer and preppie *par excellence*—arrived to share B.J. and Hawkeye's tent and snub his aristocratic nose at their plebeian jokes and anti-preppy life-styles. David Ogden Stiers, a bearish theater actor with a voice like Falstaff and a bulk to match, quickly made the role of Winchester his own and became immensely popular with viewers. His only previous sitcom experience was a featured role on the short-lived TV series *Doc*, with Barnard Hughes.

For some of the later arrivals, like Stiers and Harry Morgan, blending into the show was easy—in one sense, at least—since they were creating brand-new characters and didn't have to fear that viewers would adversely be comparing them to popular predecessors. Jamie Farr—who became the poker-playing, cigar-smoking transvestite Corporal Klinger in 1973—had the same advantage of being given entirely new material to carve out and adapt to his own talents as a performer. Gary Burghoff, on the other hand, who played Radar O'Reilly, had first originated the role in the 1970 movie, so he came to the very first rehearsal of the TV series with all of Radar's mannerisms and motivations already second nature to him. Loretta Swit, however, faced a tough challenge as Hot Lips, since Sally Kellerman, who'd played the role to perfection in the movie, had won an Oscar nomination for her performance. Moreover, the role had drawn so much attention that it had launched Sally to cinema stardom. For Loretta, it was a tough act to follow; and from the beginning, she tried to add more humanity to her portrayal of Hot Lips than Kellerman had invested in the character in the film. Gradually, over the years, she made viewers completely forget the original Hot Lips, who'd been merely a pitiful neurotic in the film, and brought warmth and sympathy to the role without abandoning any of Hot Lips' overbearing quirks.

Alan faced much the same problem in becoming Hawkeye—trying to dissociate himself from Donald Sutherland, who'd enjoyed so much success in the movie verson. M*A*S*H had launched Sutherland's cinema career; so in his first season on TV, Alan purposely went out of his way to interpret the role differently and mold Hawkeye to his own personality. He avoided the mistake of asking Twentieth Century–Fox to screen the movie for him, believing that if he watched the film he might accidentally copy Sutherland's work or try so hard not to imitate it that he'd become paralyzed as an actor. Instead, he read and reread the original Richard Hooker novel that had generated the movie screenplay, searching for bits and pieces of the character that had never been brought out in the film.

In ten years, Alan still hasn't stopped refining his characterization. As rehearsal progresses for a new episode of M*A*S*H each week, Alan continues to make script changes right up to the final taping—striving for a perfection in every scene that sometimes tests the patience of his crew and co-workers. Alan doesn't apologize for his demanding attitude on the set. "Actors going into *M*A*S*H* always knew this would never be just a nine-to-five operation," he says. Longtime co-star McLean Stevenson remembers that Alan was more intense about his performance than any actor Stevenson had ever worked with. "His concentration is incredible," Stevenson reveals. "He doesn't just act out a role. He lives and breathes it while he's on the set."

In a crazy way, what Alan adores—and dreads most—about the show are the recurring operating-room scenes. More than anyone in the cast, he wants those scenes inserted because they're a simple, fast-paced way of making the show's antiwar statement an integral part of the comic action. Yet for Alan, playing a surgeon—discussing shop talk like hemorrhaging and blood plasma and amputation—is queasy business. In 1979, Alan was chosen as guest speaker at Columbia University's College of Physicians and Surgeons graduation ceremonies, and the 210th graduating class of medical students laughed heartily when he revealed, "Personally, I'm not a great fan of blood. I don't mind people having it. I just don't enjoy seeing them wear it." In his early days at Fordham, Alan had actually contemplated a career in medicine, but his queasiness about cuts and bruises, combined with his poor grades in science, had quickly changed his mind. It was his father who'd pushed him to become a doctor, thinking that medicine was a more secure livelihood than show business. It's ironic that success and security should have come to Alan by his playing a doctor on *M*A*S*H*.

Delivering the commencement address at Columbia was, in fact, an honor that most authentic doctors would be proud to receive; even more notably, Alan was the first actor in the history of the school to be invited to speak at commencement. According to class president Alan Ross, "We wanted someone who was a humanitarian. There's no reason it has to be a doctor every year." And Alan was eager to accept because, aside from the distinguished public honor, he had strong personal reasons for attending the ceremonies. Two members of the graduating class were the children of family friends.

After regaling the audience by shattering Hawkeye's image as an imperturbable healer, Alan grew more serious for a moment and advised the students to remember one thing as they set out in the practice of medicine: "The head bone is connected to the heart bone," he said, "and don't ever let them come apart." Then, returning to his own lack of medical valor, he quipped: "I have yet to see a real operation, because the mere smell of a hospital reminds me of a previous appointment." But he maintained that as a Hollywood star, he did share at least a few similarities with doctors. "We both study the human being. And we both try to offer relief," he said. "You through medicine and I through laughter. . . . And we both charge a lot."

Ultimately, laughter is the purpose of $M*A*S*H$. Whether or not that laughter actually heals human beings is debatable, but nevertheless it's the feeling of being entertained that keeps viewers coming back week after week. Those viewers, in turn, keep Nielsen ratings high, which keeps sponsors interested in supporting the program and networks happy to keep televising it—the eternal prime-time cycle, week after week, season after season.

Sometimes, however, the best laughs are the ones the camera never captures. Playing practical jokes on each other—a routine tension-breaker on most sets—is treated almost as a religious obligation among the $M*A*S*H$ gang. Apparently, though, on one occasion

Alan went a little bit too far and wound up temporarily alienating costar Mike Farrell. Alan thought it would be a terrific gag to hide the album of family photos that Farrell kept in his dressing trailer—just the kind of stunt, in fact, that Hawkeye would pull on B.J. But Farrell was incensed that Alan had taken such liberties with his personal property and didn't calm down until a full apology was offered. Later, though, Farrell retaliated, in perfect form, by masterminding a prank that left Alan cooling his heels and muttering helplessly under his breath. Alan and Loretta Swit were on location, filming a scene where a jeep was supposed to pick them up and drive them back to the medical unit after they'd been stranded in the jungle for days. When the jeep arrived back at camp, the whole cast was supposed to give them a hero's welcome, carrying off Alda and Swit on their shoulders. Instead, Farrell got the whole gang to join him in completely sabotaging the scene. When the jeep arrived with Swit and Alda, the cast rushed out to carry off the driver shoulder-high, leaving the two stars sitting in the jeep dumbstruck. Finally, Alan and Loretta both burst out laughing too, and then, of course, the whole scene had to be reshot, adding another hour to the work day.

Even when the joke's on him, Alan doesn't get angry—at least not in front of the cast. Gary Burghoff once remarked that when Alan was incensed about a production problem, he calmly informed the producers that he was *very upset*. Burghoff, who's more fiery by nature, often marveled how he and Alan could be so infuriated by the same backstage screwup, yet Alan would refuse to lose his cool while Burghoff would invariably blow his stack. Occasionally, other members of the cast would blow up at Alan for that very reason. They mistakenly believed that his inability to scream, yell and drive his fist through the scenery meant he didn't care. The truth was, he did care deeply. But something in Alan's personality has always made him hold back emotionally in front of other people.

Eventually, Alan used that quality about himself to great advantage in *The Four Seasons*. It became a major flaw in the character of Jack Burroughs; and during a particularly heated argument with his wife Kate, she accused him of being impossible to fight with because he refused to get angry. In a strange way, Jack's obsession with being reasonable at all costs had become a weapon to make his wife feel perpetually inferior.

A former *M*A*S*H* castmate contends it can indeed be a very lethal weapon at times. "In the early days of the show," he says, "there were times when the whole cast would get enraged about a particular situation foisted on us by the studio that we considered unfair. I knew Alan was as angry as the rest of us, but he never let it show. At first, I'd get angry at myself for losing my temper on the set. But then I'd hold a grudge against Alan for days because I felt his calmness had made me look bad in front of the producers."

But Loretta Swit, who's worked closely with Alan since 1972, thinks Alan's trademark as TV's most unflappable star is really a myth. While work problems rarely get under his skin, *people* problems can send him into a quiet fury. Ill-treatment of someone on the set, any breach of kindness, can spark a harsh reaction from him; and a family problem will weigh on his mind for days. Loretta recalls seeing him in tears once, during rehearsal, right after he'd finished reading a letter from his daughter.

"But he's always in control," she told writer Joseph Bell, "because he has a kind of inner peace. He has great respect for himself as a person—and therefore great respect for other people."

Sometimes, however, that respect for other people can lead Alan to assume the role of big brother, even when his advice isn't asked for. Once he caught Wayne Rogers on a late-night talk show and something Rogers said on the air ruffled Alan's pro-feminist feathers. Rogers had jokingly referred to his wife as his "old lady" and a "great broad." Alan felt it was a derogatory way to characterize women, so he took Wayne aside on the set the next day to chew him out. On another occasion, Alan overheard Loretta Swit lacing into a new production assistant who, it turned out, had never watched *M*A*S*H* and therefore didn't understand a lot of what was happening in staging the show. Loretta felt it was a momentous gaff, but Alan ordered her to be more forgiving, telling her, "Not everyone in America watches *M*A*S*H*."

Undoubtedly, Alan Alda is a tough man to work with. His reasonableness can be exasperating. His dedication can be nerve-wracking. And at times, his own private crusades for family life, women's rights and simple kindness between people can make him appear rigid and unyielding. In Hollywood, there are two different philosophies about him. His detractors claim that he tries to be a saint, and saints are wonderful as long as you keep your distance—up close, they can be impossible to deal with. His defenders argue that he's a man who believes in things strongly, who really cares, and in his profession his humanity is rare and refreshing; naturally it makes him suspect.

One criticism leveled against *M*A*S*H*—and therefore against Alan himself since his image is tied up so strongly with the show—is the continual stream of blood and gore that characterizes script after script. It seems ironic that *M*A*S*H*, in some ways the most intelligent comedy series ever presented on television, might also be accused of featuring sensationalism and violence. But Alan maintains that *M*A*S*H* differs from any other medical show because the operation scenes deal exclusively with traumatic injuries. *M*A*S*H* shows the horrifying results of people's inflicting wounds on other people, and doesn't just select diseases at random like *Doctor Kildare* or *Ben Casey* did. The blood and gore on *M*A*S*H* also differs significantly from the kind of "unfelt violence" that most TV dramas casually indulge in. On *Hart to Hart,* for example, characters regularly die when bombs explode in their flashy sportscars or intruders spotlessly bludgeon them to death. Within minutes after learning the news, Jennifer Hart's worrying what dress to wear to dinner, while Max the cook frets in the kitchen that the quiche Lorraine is ruined. On *M*A*S*H* the violence is honest, but compassionate. Viewers see wounded soldiers suffering; but they also see the suffering of the doctors who are trying to save them.

11

When *M*A*S*H* goes on location to the 20th Century–Fox ranch in Malibu Canyon, filming begins at 7:00 A.M. The alarm clock rings earliest for Loretta Swit—the show's only female regular—who rises promptly at 4:30 A.M. to put on all her own makeup before driving to work. If she were somewhat less of a perfectionist, Loretta could leave her face entirely in the hands of the show's makeup team and get a little more beauty rest. But despite the tough facade of an Army nurse that she wears so convincingly on *M*A*S*H*—and the abrasiveness that sometimes carries over and heats up rehearsals—the brashness is only skin deep in Loretta Swit. Underneath, she still occasionally doubts herself enough to get moody and depressed. In fact, she credits Alan Alda with helping her overcome some of her worst insecurities.

The actress who's compulsively disciplined about putting on her makeup is also slightly uneasy with her own success. Even after nine seasons on *M*A*S*H*, she sometimes still signs "Sally Kellerman" when fans ask for her autograph—a joke, perhaps, or maybe a sign that she can't quite accept the fact that the role of Hot Lips is really hers.

In a sense, Loretta Swit is still proving herself. Some of the insecurity as an actress may stem from the fact that her parents fought her tooth and nail about going into show business. Raised in Passaic, N.J., she defied her Polish-American parents by leaving home to try her luck, first in New York, then in Hollywood, instead of settling down with a local boy.

Her father, an upholsterer, and her mother, a housewife, were devastated. "When I was a little girl, my mother used to take me to double features at the movies," Loretta recalls, "and sometimes we'd sit through the whole show twice. I was very shy as a child and overweight in the bargain—and movies were a terrific escape for me. As far back as I can remember, I wanted to be an actress when I grew up, even though my parents were dead set against it." Loretta's father fumed and her mother practically threw herself across the front door when Loretta left home; nevertheless she headed for New York. There she worked as a typist to pay the tuition at Gene Frankel's Theatre Workshop and barely survived in a slum apartment where rats occasionally dropped in to visit.

In 1965, she understudied the lead in the Broadway comedy *Any Wednesday*; then she toured for three years with Don Rickles and Ernest Borgnine, playing their upstairs neighbor in *The Odd Couple*. That break led to a national touring company of *Mame*, where Loretta played Agnes Gooch opposite Susan Hayward; and finally, in the late 1960s, she landed in Hollywood, making the rounds of all the prime-time drama series—from *Gunsmoke* to *Mannix*—in forgettable one-shot roles.

At first, the *M*A*S*H* producers were leery of casting her as Hot Lips. Even though she'd had terrific stage experience as a comedienne, in Los Angeles she was known mainly as a dramatic actress in westerns and detective shows. To keep her Hollywood credits from further prejudicing them, Loretta, against her agents' advice, refused to show Reynolds and Gelbart any of her *Mannix* or *Hawaii Five-O* clips. She won her *M*A*S*H* role strictly on the basis of a brand-new screen test.

After all these years on *M*A*S*H*, the real Loretta still remains an enigma to many of her colleagues. Part of her can be driving and relentless (she's been known to work a ten-hour day on the set even when suffering from a bad bout of flu); but part of her can also be zany and outrageous. Who could forget the time she snuck into a restaurant cloakroom at a cast dinner party and stashed surgical gloves filled with water in the attaché cases of a few CBS executives who were on her personal hit list?

Perhaps the co-worker who knows her best is Alan Alda. From the beginning, Alan and Loretta have enjoyed a special chemistry—an ability to operate on the same wavelength and instinctively understand and respect each other's moods. Loretta, in fact, is friendly with the entire Alda family; she even corresponds regularly with Alan's three daughters.

When Wayne Warga, a writer for the *Los Angeles Times*, inquired about her professional relationship with Alan, Loretta praised not only his acting skills, but also his occasional pinch-hitting as the show's writer and director. She confessed that some of the episodes Alan wrote were so moving that she cried the first time she read them. Her admiration for her long-running costar is obvious. "He does it all well," she told Warga, referring to Alan's triple-play success as star, author and director. Then, on a more personal level, she added, "He's proof to me that if you really work at it you can have a career and a family, and make them both successful."

Loretta Swit's remarks seem an exact echo of what another costar, Marlo Thomas, found so appealing about Alan—his enduring twenty-four-year marriage, a marriage that remains constant despite the struggles and pressures of fame. The fact that Alan can be a star and still be happily married seems to strike a responsive chord in women—especially women like Marlo Thomas and Loretta Swit, who discovered early on in their careers that pursuing stardom meant putting marriage on indefinite hold.

Loretta admits that for a long time she felt guilty about being unmarried, perhaps because of her early conditioning. She grew up believing that a woman, no matter how successful, was somehow incomplete without a husband and children. Ironically, Alan, the zealous family man, helped Loretta come to terms with her own bachelorhood, counseling her like an understanding big brother. "Alan has deep insights about women," she says. "He understands what we feel and why we feel it—the guilts and conflicts we live with. Thanks to Alan, I don't feel guilty anymore about not wanting a family. My parents and friends are my family."

It's hard to say whether Alan's feminism makes him such a compassionate friend to women, or whether his compassion is actually what sparks his feminism. At any rate, on more than one occasion, "big brother" Alan has done a little impromptu consciousness-raising on Loretta's behalf. Aside from helping her sort out her feelings about marriage—and about turning thirty-five without the possibility of children in her life—Alan has encouraged her not to be intimidated by situations where she's far outnumbered by men. The $M*A*S*H$ environment itself can often put Loretta at a distinct disadvantage. She is, after all, the

Robert Alda with his son Alan, California 1945.

Alan helps his father wire lamps, 1945. PICTORIAL PARADE

Alan's first big Broadway success, *The Owl and the Pussy-cat*, with Diana Sands, 1964. FRIEDMAN-ABELES

Alan in his first movie, *Paper Lion*, 1968.

Alan co-starred with Marlo Thomas in *Jenny*, 1970.

The original M*A*S*H gang: Larry Linville, Loretta Swit, Wayne Rogers, Alan, Gary Burghoff and McLean Stevenson.

The later M*A*S*H group: William Christopher, Jamie
Farr, David Ogden Stiers, Harry Morgan, Alan, Loretta
Swit and Mike Farrell.

Alan as Hawkeye Pierce.

Alan with his father, Robert, appearing in an episode of
M*A*S*H. U.P.I.

Alan co-starred
with
Ellen Burstyn
in the movie
version of the
Broadway hit,
*Same Time,
Next Year,*
1978.

Alan wrote, directed and starred in *The Seduction of Joe Tynan*, 1979.

Barbara Harris played Alan's wife in *Joe Tynan*.

On TV, Alan appeared with Ron Howard on the Mike Douglas Show.

Alan made himself at home on the John Davidson Show.

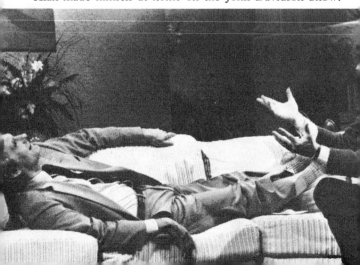

Both Robert and Alan Alda supported the actors' strike, 1980 GLOBE PHOTOS

Alan and Robert Alda with Antony Alda, Alan's half brother, at The People's Choice Awards, 1980. PICTORIAL PARA

Alan and Arlene at Nikon House, at her one-woman photography show. PICTORIAL PARADE

only female regular in the whole group, surrounded by male cameramen, male producers and male technicians.

During the early days of the show, the male-female acting ratio was a little more balanced with Linda Meiklejohn, Odessa Cleveland and Marcia Strassman all playing nurses under Hot Lips' command. But in later years, those roles faded out as the show began deemphasizing the skirt-chasing aspects of military confinement in favor of more serious dramatic themes. Occasionally, Alan, as a leading spokesman for the Equal Rights Amendment, has been criticized for not pushing for more women actors on his own show; yet certainly in his personal dealings with women, no one would ever seriously label him a sexist.

Loretta recalls that shortly after the show premiered, she and Alan found themselves roped into speaking at a press conference publicizing *M*A*S*H*. Suddenly, looking at all the photographers and reporters who'd packed the auditorium, it dawned on Loretta that she was the only woman in the room. It made her more nervous than she already was, but when she turned to Alan and pointed out the fact to him, he told her to call attention to it in the press conference. Loretta, who'd grown up believing that women aren't supposed to threaten men, found it hard to verbalize her dismay that there wasn't a single woman journalist on hand to interview her. But she followed Alan's advice and afterward felt proud of herself for voicing her new feminist convictions.

Loretta had felt the first twinges of women's lib just before joining *M*A*S*H*. Working with Jacqueline Bisset in the film *Stand Up and Be Counted*, Loretta began to suspect there was something wrong with what American culture expects women to be. It happened when she saw Jackie's emotional reaction to an item in a gossip column. At the time, Jackie was romantically involved with Michael Sarrazin, simply enjoying the ease of the relationship and not hoping it would lead to anything permanent. The columnist blithely assumed otherwise and printed a personal message to Michael—that he should give Jackie a wedding ring as a Christmas present. After all, isn't getting married, ultimately, what every woman is supposed to want? It dawned on Loretta, watching Jackie Bisset agonize over that item, how brainwashed women really are—especially since the columnist who wrote the item was a woman herself!

Working with Alan was like a breath of fresh air. A sympathetic, intelligent man, from the outset he judged her not as a woman but strictly as a person. According to *People* magazine, Loretta credits Alan with helping her channel her feelings of rage and intimidation into a healthy and more peaceful sense of self. "I think of Alan as a teacher," she says. "He is so involved in women's lib and has helped me to have confidence in myself. He is a gentle, kind man, and I owe a lot of my transformation into a liberated person to him."

Alan was, perhaps, a teacher of a different kind for his first costar, Wayne Rogers. It wasn't exactly a relationship that raised either man's consciousness, though it certainly raised a few conflicts. During his three years as Trapper John, Wayne watched Alan rise above the rest of the cast, basking in the glow of Emmy awards, publicity—all the trappings of star status—while Wayne's own sense of being an equal slowly diminished. He finally left the show in a heated legal battle with 20th Century–Fox, made an abortive comeback in a short-lived detective series called *City of Angels*, and didn't get a second chance at stardom until 1979 in *House Calls*. Pointedly enough, after his souring experience on M*A*S*H, Wayne has become a rather formidable power-grabber himself, demanding the kind of behind-the-scenes control that stars like Alan Alda are frequently accused of. On *House Calls*, Wayne reportedly gets script approval, the right to pick his own producer, and the right to help make cast selections.

During the time they actually worked together, Alan and Wayne were friendly enough on the set but far from inseparable buddies offscreen. They certainly didn't play poker and go drinking together like their TV counterparts, Hawkeye and Trapper John. In some ways, they had a great deal in common. They were both highly intelligent men with a mutual interest in establishing themselves as serious writers aside from their work as actors (Alan wrote episodes of *M*A*S*H* in his spare time; Wayne kept an unfinished novel in his typewriter at home). Yet another trait they shared—and this may have been their downfall as far as friendship was concerned—was tremendous ambition. It's a quality that makes men uneasy rivals at best. For three years they were careful not to step on each other's marks on the set or block each other's camera angles, but observers sometimes wondered how much of the politeness was truce rather than trust.

Although Wayne was an Ivy League graduate and a fan of sensitive novelists like Carson McCullers, in some ways he was a lot rougher around the edges than Alan. A lawyer's son from Birmingham, Ala., as a teenager Wayne was a self-proclaimed juvenile delinquent—drinking beer, chasing girls, flunking out of school regularly—and he finally wound up in a private academy for incorrigible kids in Bellbuckle, Miss. At Bellbuckle, he buckled down enough to impress the admissions committee at Princeton University. After graduating from Princeton as a history major, Wayne volunteered for Navy duty instead of rushing after the kind of young-executive job that his Ivy League credentials would easily have gained him.

Worse yet, after his Navy tour, he headed for Greenwich Village to study acting at the Neighborhood Playhouse—a decision that shocked and infuriated his straitlaced Southern family. Years later, even after starring on *M*A*S*H* and becoming a multimillionaire by wisely investing his TV earnings, Wayne told interviewers he was considered the black sheep of the clan. His mother still had trouble deciding if he was respectable or not.

Unlike Alan Alda, who realized at an early age that being one of the guys wasn't important to him, Wayne grew up with a much more traditional image of masculinity, and it took him a long time to accept the fact that acting was a manly profession. Wayne once confided to writer Rex Reed a painfully humorous incident from his starving-actor days that drives the point home with a vengeance. To tide him over between acting jobs, he was waiting tables at a posh Manhattan hotel. One night, a few of his old classmates from Princeton walked in and, as luck would have it, were seated at Wayne's station. Wayne was so embarrassed he hid his face behind a napkin. He told the headwaiter he felt ill and rushed out of the dining room so he wouldn't have to face his college friends.

He was embarrassed not only by his low-paying job, but by the thought that the Princetonites might discover he was an aspiring actor. "I had been playing football and basketball with these guys at Princeton, and here they were in business suits and I was studying modern dance with Martha Graham and ballet with Pearl Lang. I guess I was afraid they'd call me a fag."

Rogers got his first break in 1960, playing the lead in an ABC weekly western called *Stagecoach West.*

But the series failed, and he spent the next twelve years doing approximately three hundred guest shots on nighttime television before *M*A*S*H* came along. Undoubtedly, his high-rated stint as Trapper John opened many doors for him in Hollywood, although it took him a while to live down the publicity that ensued from his fiery exit.

Wayne maintains that dollar signs weren't his main bone of contention with 20th Century–Fox TV. Nor has he ever referred to Alan Alda's special star status as a personal irritant. Yet by the spring of 1975, when Wayne angrily took a walk, thereby earning the reputation of a troublemaker and a hot head, it seemed obvious that the producers of *M*A*S*H* weren't interested in catering to *two* high-powered male stars. Wayne claims he was dissatisfied with the show from the day he first arrived on the set. He insists that when he originally signed on as Trapper John, the producers had promised him better billing, a higher salary and eventually a share of the profits—but contractually those promises never became realities.

Still, his gripes went far beyond pure business considerations. In a 1981 interview in *TV Guide,* Wayne asserted that he felt creatively stifled during his three years on *M*A*S*H.* This sense of being undervalued angered him most, since he believed that Trapper John could have been fleshed out and humanized had anyone in control really cared. "I wasn't able to contribute beyond showing up on time, saying the words and going home," he said. "I enjoyed that, don't misunderstand me, but I was giving a hundred percent of my time and thirty percent of my creativity."

Hollywood, of course, is a peculiar world. While the producers didn't seem interested in embellishing his character or in bolstering Wayne's ego, they were equally unwilling to let him quietly exit. His farewell announcement led to a double legal battle, in which

20th Century–Fox claimed breach of contract on Wayne's part and sued him for nearly $3 million; he, in turn, immediately countersued the studio. After a great deal of hoopla, both suits were dropped. Wayne went on to do *City of Angels*, then a TV miniseries based on Irwin Shaw's book *Top of the Hill* and a feature movie, *Once in Paris*. 20th Century–Fox, meanwhile, seemed more relaxed about the loss of Wayne Rogers, once Mike Farrell settled into the cast as B.J. Hunnicutt.

Even without the kind of residuals under his belt that Alan Alda earns, Wayne went on to become as rich as if not richer than his former *M*A*S*H* mate. Today, he is reputedly worth $20 million, thanks to his being a partner in a lucrative money-management firm called Rogers and Rousso. The firm, under Wayne's aegis, handles the personal financial portfolios of such stars as Peter Falk and James Caan and—in a rather bizzare twist—the portfolio of Sherry Lansing, the president of 20th Century–Fox Productions.

Now firmly entrenched as the star of *House Calls*, Wayne seems determined to protect himself against the same kind of studio manipulations that engineered his downfall on *M*A*S*H*. This time he has everything in writing—and even what he doesn't, he apparently has no trouble simply taking. Last season, Sheldon Keller was relieved of his duties as producer of *House Calls*. His replacement was Arthur Gregory, who just happens to be Wayne Rogers' personal manager. Gregory candidly admits that Wayne—and Wayne alone—gets to see the script of every episode first, with power to demand revisions. Moreover, Wayne appears at all story conferences and production meetings, as a participant, not an observer—and his occasional clashes with the writers have been known to cause a few minor earthquakes on the set.

By the end of last season, *House Calls* seemed to be deteriorating into the same uneasy costar situation that had existed on *M*A*S*H*, except this time Wayne was definitely the star who counted. While he'd been able to obtain production and story control, his leading lady, Lynn Redgrave, found herself dismissed—and heading for a possible lawsuit—because the studio refused to meet her financial demands or allow her to breastfeed her baby daughter on the set.

Publicly and privately, Wayne tried to remove himself completely from Miss Redgrave's problems with the studio, remaining an innocent bystander in the right-to-breastfeed battle. Some observers couldn't help snickering, of course, that had the situation arisen on *M*A*S*H*, Alan Alda, a prime champion of women's rights, would have responded more forcefully on Lynn Redgrave's behalf. All that, of course, is idle conjecture. But Wayne and Alan after all these years still present very contrasting profiles in their public attitudes toward women. Occasionally, Wayne makes the kind of humorous remarks that would prompt Gloria Steinem to organize a protest rally. Since the breakup of his marriage, he no longer has occasion to refer to his former wife, Mitzi, as a "great broad," but not long ago he lamented that the onset of adolescence had hurt his daughter Laura academically. He joked that his daughter, a former straight-A student, now brings home report cards that match her bra size. She's a D cup.

Amazingly, Alan Alda finally found a friend as well as a costar in Mike Farrell, the clean-cut all-American-looking actor who replaced Wayne Rogers on *M*A*S*H*. If a computer especially designed to ferret out costar compatibility had matched them up, Alda and Farrell couldn't have hit it off better. Like Alda, Farrell was, and is, an intensely conscientious family man, a political activist and the kind of guy who goes out of his way to lower his voice and assure you he still likes you even when he is arguing with you. He was also enough of a newcomer to prime-time to willingly accept the fact that while his character B.J. Hunnicutt would stand a notch above Radar and Klinger and Colonel Potter, B.J. would never intrude on Hawkeye's well-established territory as the numero uno male on *M*A*S*H*.

Three years younger than Alan, Mike Farrell was born in St. Paul, Minn., but became a Los Angelean at the age of two when his father, a carpenter, went to work building sets for Hollywood movie studios. While Alan spent his boyhood peeking into show business through the grimy wings of burlesque theaters, Mike grew up running loose on the backlots of Paramount and MGM, captivated by the magic of fake western towns and Civil War plantations. In high school, John Wayne war movies made more of an impression on him than any of his textbooks, so, after graduation, he volunteered for the Marine Corps, although he later caught up on his education at Los Angeles City College. Later, he worked as a grocery delivery boy, while he studied acting with Jeff Corey in Hollywood and enrolled in musical-comedy classes at UCLA.

Mike was twenty-eight—and out of the Marine Corps for nine years—when he landed his first solid acting job on the NBC soap opera *Days of Our Lives*. He played a mild-mannered character named Scott Banning, married to a beautiful, discontented brunette (Susan Seaforth) who was horrible at housekeeping but an expert at infidelity. During the two years he suffered in silence on *Days of Our Lives*, the scripts called for Mike to do an inordinate amount of snoozing on the living-room couch, while Susan constantly slipped out to indulge her passion for adultery. After that, he moved into the prime-time arena, playing a young medic on the Broderick Crawford series *The Interns*, and a political aide—opposite Anthony Quinn—in *The Man and the City*, a 1971 dramatic opus about the life of a big-city mayor. Neither series, however, was successful, and Mike Farrell didn't really break into the bigtime until *M*A*S*H* came along for him in the fall of 1975.

He was nervous at first, joining a series that was already a proved success, facing a company of actors who'd been working smoothly together for three seasons. But Mike made friends quickly on the set, and his assimilation into *M*A*S*H* life was strengthened by the fact that he and Alan Alda hit it off.

Alan liked the fact that Mike was a solid family man and a concerned parent. Later on, in fact, Mike's wife, actress Judy Hayden, even turned up on the show occasionally, playing an Army nurse. Mike's children—Erin, eight, and Joshua, eleven—are considerably younger than Alan's daughters, but Alan could certainly sympathize, and even offer a few helpful hints from his own experience, when Mike fretted over how to handle a problem about their discipline or their schoolwork.

Mike tends to be more candid about his problems than Alan, but his high priority of home and hearth nevertheless won points with his *M*A*S*H* costar. Mike, for instance, who's been married for nearly twenty years, makes no bones about the fact that he and Judy have survived their share of crises. Three years after their marriage, they separated because communication between them had reached zero level. But after a year of therapy, they decided to give their marriage a second chance and both came back more committed to making their relationship work. That kind of intelligent problem-solving is a quality that Alan obviously admires.

He also admires Mike's offscreen devotion to a roster of liberal political causes that more than equals Alan's own zeal for ERA and women's rights. Mike has actively campaigned on behalf of California farm workers, civil rights, gay rights, prison reform, Democratic Presidential candidates, endangered species and the Special Olympics to benefit mentally retarded children. In 1979, when *TV Guide* wrote that if Mike Farrell ever showed up at a Republican convention "arch conservatives would boo, and Anita Bryant would probably pray for his soul," Alan couldn't have been more pleased if the words had been written about himself.

Now, after seven years of working together, their offscreen friendship is so strong that they practically breeze through their weekly buddying and bantering scenes as comrades-at-arms. Annually, Mike throws a party for the entire cast—as do Jamie Farr, Bill Christopher and Alan himself—but his nonworking get-togethers with Alan aren't restricted to big social occasions. During the filming season, when Alan is often at loose ends in L.A. without his wife Arlene, he spends a lot of time at Mike's house, where he feels welcome and comfortable. "Alan and I really care about each other," Mike says. "Even when the show's on hiatus for a few months and he's off making a movie or back in New Jersey with his family, we make it a point to stay in touch."

In seven seasons, *M*A*S*H* has opened more doors for Mike Farrell than he ever dreamed possible. He's starred in a formidable list of sophisticated and compelling TV movies—like *Battered, Letters from Frank*, and *Sex and the Single Parent*—and, following Alan's lead and encouragement, begun contributing several scripts of his own to *M*A*S*H*. More than any other cast member, Mike's progress on the show has refuted any rumors to the contrary that Alan Alda has problems sharing the spotlight. Over the years, B.J. has grown as a character to the point where he rivals Hawkeye's popularity, yet Mike continues to enjoy a closeness with Alan—and a freedom to gain his own special perks on *M*A*S*H*, like writing occasional scripts, that had eluded Wayne Rogers.

Wayne Rogers wasn't the only regular to drop out of active duty on *M*A*S*H* because of artistic differences with the show's hierarchy. After five seasons, Larry Linville asked for an honorable discharge, too. Linville became a backstage casualty because he felt that his character—cranky, ineffectual Major Frank Burns—was merely a slapstick wimp rather than anything even vaguely resembling a real human being. Hawkeye, Hot Lips and even Klinger all had their recurring moments of nobility in the script, but season after season, Major Burns served only one purpose—to be the butt of other characters' jokes. "I was very proud to be associated with *M*A*S*H*," Linville said after leaving the hit series with no clear-cut career destination in sight. "I was proud to have worked on a program that maintained such high quality, that—dramatically—was light-years ahead of any other show on the air. But the trouble was that the producers' insistence on quality was only on the other characters. Major Burns was just a foil for other people's jokes. After five seasons, I'd done everything possible with him, considering that he was still a pretty unrealistic character. The writers had turned him into a cartoon."

Linville, following Wayne Rogers and McLean Stevenson, was the third key actor to desert *M*A*S*H* under a cloud of failed contract negotiations. None of these departures ever threatened the show's ratings, yet once again rumors of backstage friction and unhappiness abounded. Why did Alan Alda, the undisputed star of the show, seem to have so much trouble coexisting with some of the show's most talented supporting players?

Linville's artistic differences with M*A*S*H were so strong that he didn't even wait for another network to sign him up before taking his walking papers. He spent an entire year after leaving M*A*S*H searching for prime-time work, living off residuals and, in a complete retreat from the pressures of show business, building a glider in his own backyard. Tinkering with experimental airplanes had been a lifelong hobby, he later explained. But in that year, 1977, the hobby became a kind of personal therapy—like basketweaving, he joked—to help him forget his career troubles.

In 1978, he returned to prime-time, costarring in the Jack Albertson sitcom *Grandpa Goes to Washington.* This time Linville was cast as a two-star general—a big step up from his role as a mere major on M*A*S*H. At first, Larry was leery of being typecast as an Army man again. He would have preferred playing a murderer, a drug addict, or a detective—anything to break the mold—but NBC promised him that his role, as Jack Albertson's son, would have a lot of humanity to it, and not just be a military stick figure. But the promotion and the promise of compelling scripts never had a chance to materialize. The series was an early victim of cancellation in that season's Nielsen war.

Since then, Larry has guest starred on nighttime series like *Love Boat* and *Fantasy Island,* but never hooked permanently into a series of his own. His personal life has been equally unsettled. Larry and his second wife, actress Vana Tribbey, are currently in the process of getting a friendly divorce, after five years of marriage.

Harry Morgan came to the role of Colonel Sherman Potter by a rather circuitous route. In the 1974 season, he appeared in a single episode of M*A*S*H as a visiting military bigwig, suffering from a slight case of insanity, who tried to have Hawkeye court-martialed. The episode was called "The General Flipped at Dawn," and Morgan's portrayal of the cuckoo Army commander eventually brought him an Emmy nomination for best single performance by a supporting actor in a series.

Morgan didn't realize it at the time, but that episode turned out to be the screen test that got him a permanent assignment with the 4077th. When McLean Stevenson left the show in the spring of 1975, the producers immediately thought of Harry Morgan as the ideal replacement because he'd been so memorable his first time out on *M*A*S*H*. And so when Colonel Henry Blake's plane crashed enroute to the States, the character of Colonel Sherman Potter was born—and Harry Morgan became the latest addition to the all-star cast.

A native of Detroit, Harry was christened Henry Bratsburg at birth; but later, as a young Hollywood actor, he decided to shorten his name, since Bratsburg didn't have the melodious ring of Garfield or Gable. So he changed it to Henry Morgan, but that only confused things more since there was already a popular radio comic named Henry Morgan. Therefore, Henry became Harry Morgan.

When Harry accepted a weekly role on *M*A*S*H*—his eighth television series—he immediately assured a place for himself in the record books. No other actor had ever starred in that many prime-time programs. (His other series were *December Bride, Pete and Gladys, Kentucky Jones, The Richard Boone Show, Dragnet, The D.A.* and *Hec Ramsey*.)

His first season as a full-fledged *M*A*S*H* regular, Harry worried about a viewer backlash over McLean Stevenson's departure. He recalled that Ken Curtis, who replaced Dennis Weaver on *Gunsmoke*, took years to work into the rolé and regularly got irate fan letters that read, "Get rid of Festus—we want Chester back!" Morgan's worries didn't diminish any when, a few weeks after Colonel Potter's debut, he was accosted by a M*A*S*H fan and his wife in a Los Angeles restaurant. Barely polite, they told him, "We really liked Henry Blake—so you'd better be good and you'd better be funny!"

But after working in twenty-five motion pictures, seven TV series and numerous Broadway shows, Morgan thought he could face the challenge and handle it. He was particularly excited about joining the crew of the 4077th because he'd been very impressed by the on-set atmosphere when he'd done "The General Flipped at Dawn." There was a genuine friendliness among the cast that's a rarity on most TV shows, where bickering and pettiness usually account for more time lost during rehearsal than waiting for lights and cameras to be reset.

Morgan immediately developed a rapport with Alan Alda, perhaps because he, like Alda and Mike Farrell, is also a devoted family man. Married since 1940, Harry and his wife Eileen have four sons and five grandsons. Now, after seven years on M*A*S*H—with an astounding number of Emmy nominations—he feels very comfortable with the role, and nearly everyone in the cast looks up to him in an affectionate, fatherly way. "We have so much fun sitting around off-camera that it really doesn't change when we get on camera," he told Jerry Buck in the Los Angeles Herald-Examiner. "There's a lot of affection flowing around here."

David Ogden Stiers is another case of a replacement who seems to have filled the shoes of his M*A*S*H predecessor. His character, Major Charles Emerson Winchester III, was invented to step into the empty stuffed shirt vacated by Larry Linville as

Major Frank Burns. But Stiers has possibly more than filled out the shirt—he's given the role a warmth and humanity that buffoons rarely display on prime time; and offscreen, Stiers himself is a far cry from the pompous, bombastic Winchester. During rehearsal breaks, he skateboards down the streets of the 20th Century–Fox Studio, and when security guards try to stop him, Stiers sticks out his tongue as he gleefully whizzes by at twenty-five miles an hour.

Producer Burt Metcalf thought Stiers might be right for the Winchester role after catching him on several episodes of *The Mary Tyler Moore Show*. He'd played a "lovably unlovable" thorn in the side of station WJM, and Metcalfe's instincts told him it was just the right quality for Hawkeye's new nemesis.

Stiers and Alda, who share a passion for classical theater, have become famous on the set for their rambling and involved Shakespearean discussions. In fact, David, prior to *M*A*S*H*, had played—and triumphed in—some of the great stage roles that Alan once dreamed of tackling. As a member of the Shakespeare Festival in Santa Clara, California, he played Richard III, Polonius and King Lear, twice. But Shakespeare isn't the only diversion during a long day of shooting on *M*A*S*H*. David has been known to mediate some hilarious disputes between castmates, like the time that Mike Farrell hid Alan Alda's bicycle.

But *M*A*S*H* is a set where no one, not even mediators who've also played King Lear, are safe from being the butt of an occasional prank. Stiers once came back from a four-day vacation to find his dressing room had been "redecorated"—in screaming shades of orange and purple paint—in his absence. He never was able to apprehend the culprits, but Loretta Swit and Mike Farrell had rather guilty grins on their faces for several days after the incident.

Winchester may bellow like Falstaff, but the character on M*A*S*H who most closely approached "tragedy" was Radar O'Reilly, the short, four-eyed enlisted man who hardly seemed a fit candidate for Boy Scout camp, let alone the Korean War. Over the years, some of the show's most poignant scripts involved Radar, the timid recruit who'd been drafted into uniform before he ever had a chance to grow out of adolescence back in Iowa. In the very first season, an episode called "Love Story" showed Radar devastated by a "Dear John" letter that came in the form of a record, while Hawkeye and Trapper tried—and failed—to cure Radar's depression by matching him up with a new girl. Later on, in another painful episode, Radar won an instant promotion to lieutenant in a barracks poker game, only to find himself so terrified by the thought of being an officer that he gladly reneged on his new responsibilities. A running emotional undercurrent on the show involved Radar's homesickness, poignantly underlined in letters home to his mother in Iowa and in the fuzzy home movies of farm happenings she sent back to him.

In 1979, when Gary Burghoff left the show, Radar's departure was covered in a special two-part episode. Klinger, who took over Radar's job as the company radio officer, had a tough time filling Radar's shoes (though he certainly dressed a lot more flashily). When the hospital generator broke down, making it impossible for the doctors to perform surgery on critically wounded patients, Klinger couldn't cut through military red tape to get a new generator delivered. Colonel Potter grew increasingly disgusted with Klinger's ineptitude; and finally Klinger railed back at him, "I'm not Radar—and you'll just have to get used to me!" The double episode showed how deeply, from Col. Potter right down the line, all the M*A*S*H officers missed Radar. For all his timidity and milquetoast qualities, he'd been a master at slicing bureaucratic red tape. The unit could barely function without him.

Off the set, Gary Burghoff was also sorely missed by the cast. When Gary left, the crew lost one of their best poker players and the cast lost one of their most sensitive, considerate talents. Week after week, he'd go out of his way to adjust his own performance during rehearsal so he could back up, rather than steal, a scene from another star. At cast parties, he'd entertain the rest of the gang with songs he'd written himself (he's a professional songwriter with over a hundred tunes to his credit); and on his dressing-room mirror he'd tape original poems that he regularly made up about the joy of working on *M*A*S*H*. The juvenile qualities that he invested in Radar were just an acting trick, but the gentleness and sensitivity were real.

Gary Burghoff originally created the role of Radar in the movie version of *M*A*S*H*, after director Robert Altman spotted him in the Los Angeles production of *You're a Good Man, Charlie Brown*. As the charmingly sad-sack title character in the musical, Gary seemed perfect for the Chaplinesque role of Radar. Prior to that, the young actor—stymied by his height and puckish appearance—had found only sporadic success in show business. In fact, not too long before he landed the role of Charlie Brown in the original off-Broadway production, he was still selling men's underwear at a Fifth Avenue department store.

During his long run on the TV series, Radar's role was expanded considerably, giving Gary a chance to play tears as well as laughter. In episodes where Radar's mom sent home movies to her son, Gary actually put on a wig and dress and padded his chest to impersonate Radar's stout, befuddled and equally four-eyed mother. Perhaps the hardest scene he ever played on M*A*S*H occurred in the final episode of the 1974-75 season, when news came that Colonel Henry Blake's plane had been shot down over the Sea of Japan. McLean Stevenson was actually Gary's closest friend on the show, and he was on the set that day, watching Gary read the announcement of Blake's death to the rest of the medical unit. The raw emotion that Gary brought to the scene had more realism to it than viewers suspected. As Gary read the Army bulletin, he caught sight of McLean standing just a few feet away, and he choked up completely, realizing that they'd never work together again on M*A*S*H.

As Radar, Gary was nominated for a supporting actor Emmy seven times—in fact, every season that he appeared on the show. In May 1978 (his fifth time out), Gary actually won the Emmy, and since he wasn't present at the ceremonies, buddy Alan Alda came onstage to accept on Gary's behalf. Alan's genuine pleasure at Gary's victory was written all over his face. He informed the audience that Gary was a "wonderful, gifted and sensitive actor," then quipped that it was a good thing that Gary had missed out on his own night of triumph because he would have been too shy to publicly pat himself on the back like that.

Like most of the M*A*S*H regulars, Gary made strong friendships backstage that survived even after he left. When Gary became a father for the first time, he turned to Alan Alda and Mike Farrell for tips on parenthood—in fact, he stills gets in touch with them when family problems arise. And when his own father passed away, Gary drew especially close to Harry Morgan, who, as Radar's boss on M*A*S*H, had been an onscreen fatherly figure to him for four seasons.

William Christopher plays a different kind of father on *M*A*S*H*, Father Mulcahy, the reticent, easygoing Army chaplain. Although Bill's been with the show since the opening episode, he wasn't granted "regular" status for a long time because the producers weren't sure if Father Mulcahy would develop into a permanent fixture. They'd had a lot of trouble figuring out what kind of priest Father Mulcahy should be, and then an even worse time finding a suitable actor for the role. Bill Christopher hadn't been chosen for the TV pilot. He was only called in a few days before the first episode was taped when the original Father Mulcahy had to be fired.

Bill came to *M*A*S*H* after a rather second-string career in prime-time television, though he caught the producer's eye because he'd recently made a few appearances on *The Carol Burnett Show*. Even after his first few years on *M*A*S*H*, he was still low man on the totem pole—scriptwise—and viewers were hardly passionately attached to his character. But in recent seasons, Father Mulcahy has begun playing a slightly more prominent role. In 1979, in a script called "An Eye for a Tooth," the good father finally had his moment of glory when an entire episode explored a compelling personal crisis in his life. The show opened with Mulcahy trying to hide his feelings of disappointment at being passed over for promotion. His deep sense of humiliation was further compounded as he watched a helicoptor pilot get an instant promotion for an act of battlefront heroism. Mulcahy began to question his value to the Army as a man of the cloth and nearly endangered his life trying to act more like a combat soldier than a priest. It was, perhaps, one of the best *M*A*S*H* episodes ever aired, exploring both the priest's crisis of faith and the man's feelings of frustration at being perennially overlooked and unrewarded.

Backstage, however, Bill Christopher is far from overlooked. A family man, like most of the show's regulars, Bill and his wife Barbara are the parents of two teenage sons, and throw an annual cast party at their home that's one of the eagerly awaited highlights of the *M*A*S*H* filming season. Perhaps the quietest member of the gang, Bill can usually be seen sitting near the set during rehearsal breaks reading Latin or Greek, a form of relaxation that eases his tension the way other people escape into crossword puzzles. Bill's chair has become such a studio landmark that, naturally, at some point it had to become the outlet for a Loretta Swit–Mike Farrell practical joke. When Bill was hospitalized for several weeks with a bout of hepatitis, his castmates decided on the perfect welcome-back gift. In his absence, they painted Bill's chair a sickly shade of yellow—to match the color of his face.

There have been times, though, in the show's history, when faces have paled for reasons other than illness. And, practical jokes aside, the atmosphere on the set was no laughing matter. Nobody ever left *M*A*S*H* with more of a bang than a whimper than McLean Stevenson.

On McLean's last day of filming, Loretta Swit and Gary Burghoff both burst into tears; but over at the 20th Century–Fox executive offices, the mood was probably different. From the time he started on *M*A*S*H*, McLean had been rebellious, loud and uncompromising. To the actors, he was often a backstage hero, airing valid gripes about working conditions that nearly everyone shared with him but were too timid to argue on their own behalf. McLean, never the kind of guy to sit still when his personal sense of justice was piqued, had become the cast crusader. Unfortunately, crusaders, whether they're tilting at windmills in Washington or Hollywood, generally wind up perched on a very fragile pedestal.

McLean had been a rather singleminded kid even back is his native Illinois. Although his father was chairman of the local draft board, McLean stubbornly refused to accept active duty in World War II, because the thought of killing anyone sickened him. Luckily, he was able to land an assignment with a paramedical troop, serving out his hitch in the war tending casualties, much like his future TV troops on *M*A*S*H* would do. His personal experience in a military medical unit turned out to be great preparation for *M*A*S*H*, but like Alan Alda, McLean had only hardened his own pacifist views in his Army stint. Years later, he acidly joked that he lived through World War II in a permanent state of "morning sickness," throwing up every time he had to nurse a badly wounded soldier.

He may have been a sensitive soul on the battlefront, but he proved a lot tougher on the *M*A*S*H* set. He was bumping heads with the producers right from the start, and backstage skirmishes never ceased. He almost didn't return to the show after the second season, even though he had signed a five-year contract with 20th Century–Fox. At that time, the producers sweetened the pot considerably (reportedly his salary was doubled to keep him from leaving the 4077th without a commander-in-chief). The trouble was that McLean's discontent wasn't really financial in nature, and during his third and final year on *M*A*S*H*, backstage tensions exploded into real combat.

Stevenson, along with most of the crew, was appalled by the general working conditions. Although *M*A*S*H* by this time was a major television hit, earning enormous profits for the network and the studio, the cast toiled in a far from luxurious atmosphere. In July and August, the summer heat, combined with the hot lights and camera equipment, sent the temperature onstage to a grueling 110 degrees, and there was no air-conditioning system to cool things down. On location, the sun, dust and primitive accommodations were even worse. There was only one bathroom in the makeup department for all the stars, grips and gofers to use. During breaks on location, the cast couldn't even retire to a shady place to escape the glare of the sun. Finally, after the whole cast nearly went on strike, 20th Century–Fox set up a tent for the actors to huddle in between scenes.

McLean was astounded when he tried to fight for air-conditioned dressing trailers for the show's regulars and got turned down. In this case, the show's producers were on the actors' side, but met with the same resistance themselves from a very budget-conscious studio bookkeeping department.

The final straw broke during McLean's third season when the cast was bundled off on location to a remote area in Santa Monica. They arrived shortly after sunrise and found conditions that made them want to get right back in their cars and return home. During the night a frost had accumulated on the ground and the temperature had fallen to just below freezing. There was a shortage of bathroom facilities (not to mention hot water—which meant no one could even make coffee to warm up). McLean took one look at the location site and informed the director he was leaving. He drove to a local diner a few miles away to have coffee, then phoned 20th Century–Fox with an ultimatum: He'd stay at the diner all day if he had to—no matter how much money he cost the studio by disrupting the filming—until an executive came to the diner to discuss the situation.

Bill Self, head of television production for 20th Century–Fox, managed to calm McLean down over the phone, and a while later he actually left the diner and returned to work. But after that incident, he was obviously a marked man. At the end of the season, the studio eagerly let him out of his unfinished contract; and, in a particularly snide, self-protective move, purposely ordered the character of Henry Blake killed, so that McLean could never return to the role in another television series.

His last day on Stage 9, McLean watched Gary Burghoff film the scene announcing his death, then quietly walked to his dressing room to pack his bags and get out. Suddenly, three years of pent-up emotion caught up with him and he cried. In fact, he was so distraught that he went straight home, instead of appearing at his own farewell party that had been arranged by the cast.

Since then, McLean Stevenson has negotiated a number of promising prime-time deals that all, for one reason or another, failed to equal his *M*A*S*H* success. In December 1976, he starred in his own NBC series, *The McLean Stevenson Show*, playing a hardware-store owner in Evanston, Ill., fielding the comic complications caused by a wife, two grown daughters, assorted grandchildren and a mother-in-law. This midseason replacement show was canceled the following spring; and his next venture, *In the Beginning*, proved even more disastrous. In this 1978 CBS comedy series, McLean was cast as a conservative priest trying to run a storefront ghetto mission with a very liberated nun (Priscilla Lopez). The show aired on September 20 and was canceled, because of low ratings, one month later. After that, McLean returned to NBC in *Hello, Larry*, playing single parent to a pair of wily and with-it teenage daughters; and while this vehicle lasted longer than any of his previous efforts, *Hello, Larry* eventually went the way of most recent NBC shows—into Nielsen oblivion.

The constant battles with studio brass over working conditions probably caused McLean Stevenson to join the 4077th casualty list, while Wayne Rogers and Larry Linville left in a huff because their supposedly pivotal roles dwindled in stature over the years. Jamie Farr, on the other hand, would probably have been initially grateful for a walk-on—for which he'd had to stand and wait for hours in the broiling sun! He was a depressed, starving thirty-six-year-old actor when his agent wangled him a one-shot on *M*A*S*H* as Corporal Maxwell Klinger, a phony transvestite. That was in 1973. No one, least of all Jamie himself, ever expected that 20th Century–Fox would still be outfitting him in combat boots and Joan Crawford dresses nine years later.

The 4077th was always a haven for the mildly insane, what with Hawkeye's private liquor still set up in "The Swamp" and Radar toting his teddy bear around instead of a rifle. But their idiosyncrasies pale beside Klinger, the maddest of them all. A cigar-smoking, poker-playing "regular" guy, he arrived on *M*A*S*H* swathed in his outrageous female getups. He was vainly trying to convince his superiors that he was sexually deranged, thereby gaining a "section eight"—a medical discharge from the Army. After nine seasons, it's still a hopeless ploy. Colonel Potter, his commanding officer, is perfectly content to let Klinger wobble around in his high heels and show up at mess call wearing a diamond tiara, as long as he doesn't sashay off guard duty to fix a run in his stockings.

Over the years, Klinger has emerged as one of the

most popular, and funniest, characters on M*A*S*H. Ironically, Jamie Farr, who's responsible for playing the most militarily unfit member of the bunch, is the only cast member who ever saw active service in Korea. Although he missed combat duty in the Korean War by a few years, Jamie spent two years stationed with the Army in postwar Korea and Japan in the mid-1950s. However, his cousin, James J. Jabara, did earn a footnote in military history, as the first American flying ace of the Korean War.

Born in Toledo, Ohio, and christened Jameel Farah by his Lebanese-American parents, Jamie grew up in moderate circumstances. His father was a butcher, his mother a seamstress. In grade school, Jamie clerked in his father's shop to earn pocket money. At the age of eleven, he won $2 in a local talent contest, but he was too busy being an all-round achiever to think exclusively of a career in show business. In high school, along with being a leading force behind the drama-club variety shows, he was class president, editor of the school paper, and a varsity tennis player. In fact, Jamie was voted the most outstanding student of his graduating class at Woodward High and was elected to the National Honor Society.

Unlike Alan Alda, young Jamie didn't dare dream of someday playing roles like Hamlet and Othello. If anything, he realized his only hope as a serious actor was maybe a starring role in *Cyrano de Bergerac*. His enormous hooked nose—reminiscent of Jimmy Durante's schnozzola—pretty much ruled him out as a leading man. Nevertheless, after high school, Jamie headed for Hollywood, studied at the Pasadena Playhouse and landed a featured role in the 1955 movie *Blackboard Jungle*. After his Army stint, he became a regular on *The Red Skelton Show*, made a few more movies (like *No Time for Sergeants*), but mostly spent his time on the Los Angeles unemployment line, saving all his spare change to buy a can of tuna for dinner.

In 1963, he married Joy Ann Richards, a model (they have two children, Jonas, now twelve, and Yvonne, nine). Like Alan Alda, Jamie, as husband and family man, endured such long, dry career spells that he knew how precious success was when it finally came along. In the 1960s, he had a small role in *The Greatest Story Ever Told* and, for a while, was part of the comedy ensemble on *The Danny Kaye Show*. But mainly he did odd jobs to pay the rent and save his sanity—working as a delivery boy, a postal clerk and even an animal keeper at a chinchilla ranch, where he scooped up the poop in the cages.

As Jamie puts it, "I've been in show business for nearly thirty years, and for seventeen of them—more than half my career—I basically didn't work. When *M*A*S*H* came along offering me a regular job on the most popular show in America, was I grateful? Let me tell you, grateful wasn't the word!"

But after his first smash year on *M*A*S*H*, Jamie almost lost the success he'd waited so long to grasp. When his agent went to 20th Century–Fox to renegotiate Jamie's contract, Jamie's representative and the studio mouthpiece couldn't come to terms. Jamie's agent said his client couldn't sign the kind of contract that 20th Century–Fox was offering. That infuriated the studio man, who threatened that if Jamie didn't resign, he'd get 20th Century to boycott the agent's entire client list. No actor who used Jamie's agent would ever work for the studio again.

While his agent sulked and fumed, Jamie decided to take matters into his own hands. He went to the studio prop department, temporarily absconded with a plastic .45 revolver and marched up to the recalcitrant executive's office. Jamie kicked the door open and stormed into the room unannounced. When his nemesis looked up, he nearly had a coronary on the spot, seeing Jamie brandishing a gun at him, poised to shoot. "Listen, you louse," Jamie roared, "either you write up a contract on my agent's terms or you're a dead duck!"

The executive instantly hid under his desk, while Jamie burst out laughing. When the poor guy realized it was just a gag, he crept out from under his desk and began laughing too. Luckily for Jamie, it turned out that the exec had a sense of humor. In fact, the guy was so delighted with the stunt that his hard-line bargaining pose softened considerably. Afterwards, 20th Century—Fox graciously agreed to reopen contract talks and the matter was settled in Jamie's favor.

Perhaps Jamie Farr has succeeded in gaining clout, where others on M*A*S*H have failed, precisely because he doesn't come on like gangbusters. He found a humorous way to get his message across, rather than embroiling himself in a hopeless web of accusations and counteraccusations. "The studios are tyrannical, nobody would deny that," one knowledgeable observer says, "but actors can be just as stubborn. They get on a hit series and their egos just blow sky-high. Everybody's under incredible pressure in prime-time television—the stars, the networks, the studios. Diplomacy, not tantrums, gets people a lot further ahead."

Nevertheless, even a relatively tactful and accommodating castmember like Jamie Farr is considered expendable—and Jamie knows it. Reputedly, 20th Century—Fox long ago commissioned a script which to this day is kept in the studio vault as insurance in case Jamie takes a powder. The script is called "Klinger Finally Gets His Section Eight." Is there also a script secretly hidden somewhere in the studio called

"Hawkeye Gets His Discharge," in case Alan Alda ever leaves the series? "If so," one observer believes, "that script was probably written by Alan himself and would be the final episode of *M*A*S*H*."

12

"Alan makes a lousy star. In his position, his name should be in the columns and he should be taking girls named Jill to Acapulco. Instead, he is mad about his wife, mad about his children and mad about his house in New Jersey."

That verdict was rendered by Don Weiss, a close friend of Alan's and a director of *M*A*S*H*, who couldn't think of anything spicy to dish out about Alan when *Newsweek* sent a reporter to the *M*A*S*H* set in 1974.

In the seven years since then, no one else has unearthed anything sensational in Alan's private life, either. Although he's worked intimately with some of the most intelligent and attractive women Hollywood has to offer—stars like Marlo Thomas, Meryl Streep and Jane Fonda—Alan Alda remains serenely untempted, a rigorous nonindulger, in the most notoriously promiscuous profession in America. He is exactly what he seems: a faithful family man, not only married to the same woman for over twenty-four years, but apparently still crazy about her.

Probably the most sensational thing you can say

about Alan Alda is that he enjoys the company of women—prefers it, in fact, to the company of men. This may stem from childhood when Alan, because of his father's career and his bout with polio, was isolated from boys his own age. In school, it seemed to him, the other guys spoke a language he didn't understand or care very much about. If you didn't know sports, then you were left out. Alan, interested in books and ideas, thought most of the other guys were intellectually shallow; and his sense of apartness actually helped him communicate with girls and understand them better than most boys do. Even today, he believes that women in general make far more interesting conversationalists than men.

Perhaps that explains why Alan maintains easy and relaxed friendships with women other than his wife, without the hint of sexual infidelity ever intruding. Maureen Anderman, who played Alan's secretary in the movie *The Seduction of Joe Tynan*, remembers that one night on location in Baltimore, she and a girlfriend treated Alan and director Jerry Schatzberg to dinner. They discussed the Broadway season and mutual friends like Julie Harris, and spent a few hours of pleasant shop talk away from the pressures of the set. Maureen, whose own beau is television actor Frank Converse, remembers her experience of working with Alan as happy and low-keyed. Here was a kind and generous man who went out of his way to be friendly to minor members of the *Joe Tynan* cast, with whom you could discuss things earnestly and intelligently, without sexual tensions complicating the atmosphere. Longtime friends like Marlo Thomas and Carol Burnett would vouch for this, too: Alan is so devoted to his wife that flirtation is the farthest thing from his mind. He can be interested in other women precisely because he isn't *interested* in other women.

Paul Newman was once asked how he manages to stay faithful to Joanne Woodward—when the motion-picture business breeds unfaithfulness as roses breed thorns—and Newman philosophically replied, "Why go out for hamburger when you've got steak at home?" It's a notion that Alan Alda could thoroughly agree with.

In Alan's eyes, no woman is more remarkable than Arlene Weiss, the engaging, talented brunette from the Bronx who stole his heart twenty-five years ago. Unlike Alan, who grew up surrounded by colorful larger-than-life show types, Arlene was the product of middle-class Jewish parents. Her father was a lithographer, her mother a dressmaker; and the Weisses, like most Jewish families of the 1940s and '50s, believed that hard work, study and marrying a nice boy with a good future was the way for a daughter to get ahead. Philosophically, they weren't that different than the Aldas—especially Alan's grandparents, who'd urged his father to enroll at NYU and make something out of himself. But Alan's father had struck it rich in a business that had skyrocketed him right out of the New York ghetto, and Alan's music-hall and movieland childhood was light-years away from anything Arlene's family in the Bronx could imagine or understand. Alan's early years were like a page out of Walter Winchell's gossip column; the only celebrities Arlene Weiss saw were faces on the screen at the neighborhood Loew's movie theater.

Culturally, though, the Weiss home was a stimulating place; art and intellect were appreciated. In high school, Arlene began to play the clarinet; later, she majored in music at New York's Hunter College. After graduating Phi Beta Kappa, Arlene won a Fulbright scholarship to study at the Cologne Conservatory of Music in Germany.

In the summer of 1955, Alan was returning from

Europe when he struck up a shipboard acquaintance with a chamber-music conductor. Back in New York, she invited him to a concert at her home, where Arlene, who'd finished her studies and joined the National Orchestral Association, was one of the performers. During the party, their actual encounter, in the hostess' kitchen, was memorable, if messy. A cake that was scheduled to be dessert later that night had just fallen off the top of the refrigerator. All the other guests, walking by and eyeing the wrecked masterpiece, simply tried to avoid stepping into a pile of frosting. Arlene and Alan, both less inhibited than the rest of the highbrow crowd, sat down on the floor and started munching the cake. "Everyone else thought we were a little crazy," Alan recalls, "but Arlene and I didn't care. We just sat on the floor, swimming in frosting like two kids in a sandbox, and laughed and laughed."

In 1957, when Alan went off to be a raw recruit at Fort Benning, Georgia, Arlene spent a season with the Houston Symphony Orchestra as a clarinetist under the direction of famed conductor Leopold Stokowski. As soon as his six-month Army hitch was over, Alan hurried to Houston so he and Arlene could be married.

In 1957, the fact that Alan was Catholic and Arlene was Jewish weighed more heavily in their families' minds than it probably would today. In those days, interfaith marriages were far less common, and it took some intricate religious maneuvering to solve the gap between them.

In the end, it was Arlene who bowed to Alan's faith—a rare thing for a Jewish girl from the Bronx to do. She later explained to *Good Housekeeping* reporter Joseph N. Bell how the decision came about: "I'm a Jew, brought up nonreligious but conscious of my own background and heritage. When I met Alan, he was a practicing Catholic, who had been raised in a pretty liberal household and educated by Jesuits. When we got married, it was more important to him to be married in the church than for me not to be."

Possibly not alienating Alan from his Catholic faith was a concession to his mother, who'd endured so many other emotional blows shortly before that. Her husband of twenty-five years had deserted her and now Alan, her only child, was leaving, getting married at the age of twenty-one and establishing a home of his own. In a sense, both her husband and her son had deserted her. For Alan to openly abandon his Catholic roots by marrying a Jewish girl and following her faith just might have been too painful for Joan.

While Alan was at Fort Benning, Ga., Arlene actually took instruction in Catholicism, studying with a priest, in preparation for her conversion. And at the time of the marriage, she agreed that their children would be raised as Catholics, so that she and Alan could receive the blessings of the church.

But Arlene, never a religious girl herself, had serious doubts about wholeheartedly embracing her husband's faith. During her instruction, she raised questions that the priest couldn't answer to her satisfaction; and after their marriage, she and Alan never really considered themselves a Catholic family. Alan, who'd become impressed with existentialist philosophy during his college years, had his own serious doubts about the concepts of heaven, hell, God and immortality. About two years after their marriage, he and Arlene abandoned Catholicism completely. As he later said, "I turned away from any formal association with the church. It had been a very important part of my life before, but by then I could no longer accept some of the concepts I was told I had to accept to be a good Catholic."

In raising their three daughters, Alan and Arlene steered them away from formal Sunday-school training in any faith—believing that identifying with a single faith "gives you a sense of belonging but also a lot of guilt." Instead, the Aldas tried to give their daughters an involvement in the traditions and joy of both their backgrounds, by celebrating both Hanukkah and Christmas, for example, as holidays of love and giving and goodwill.

Alan and Arlene had launched into marriage as impulsively as they'd both ravaged that toppled cake on the night of their first meeting. Just out of the Army, Alan's employment prospects were far from hopeful when they became newlyweds; but instinctively, from the beginning, they knew their marriage would work, no matter how much they had to struggle financially. Whether they were following the Catholic custom that starting a family is a married couple's highest aspiration or the Jewish tradition that babies bring their own kind of *mazel* or a little bit of both, Alan and Arlene didn't wait for their financial picture to brighten before plunging into parenthood. Alan was a struggling actor, more often driving a cab than working onstage, when daughter Eve arrived on December 18, 1958; Elizabeth was born twenty months later on August 20, 1960; and slightly less than one year later, Beatrice arrived on August 10, 1961.

During the early years, money, or rather the lack of it, was a definite problem. Arlene used to keep a set of envelopes in her desk, marked "Food," "Rent," and "Utilities." Every night when Alan would come home after driving a cab for eight hours, he'd hand over his tips and Arlene would put a little bit of the tip money into each envelope. They hardly needed a checking account in those days because there were precious few items—aside from necessities for the children and themselves—that they could afford to buy.

Had the Aldas been a struggling young couple in 1980 instead of 1960, they probably would have approached their situation differently and become a two-career family. But Arlene wasn't crazy about the idea of turning her babies over to day-care centers, even though she could have easily gotten a decent-paying job with a symphony orchestra. Furthermore, at the time of their marriage, they'd tacitly agreed that Alan's career would come first, and for the next twenty years all their decisions as a family were made on that premise.

Looking back on the early structure of his marriage, Alan—the outwardly ardent feminist—admits he didn't always put his male ego where his mouth was. Arlene, after all, gave up a good job in Houston, in her chosen career, to move back to New York, where Alan needed to be for professional reasons. Over the years, she continually reassured him that the sacrifice wasn't really a sacrifice, because it was a decision they came to jointly. Yet in retrospect, Alan still feels they were too husband-oriented at that point. "I could have looked for a job with a theater company in Houston and sacrificed my dream of going to Broadway," he says, "but it never seriously entered our thinking. We were a young couple of the 1950s, when a husband and wife just assumed that the man's work mattered more. I wonder if we'd feel the same way if we were just starting out now."

Of course, Arlene could have hung on to her concert career. With her salary as a musician, combined with Alan's income as an actor, their financial picture would have brightened considerably; and they could easily have afforded babysitters. But the idea of leaving their children in the care of hired help didn't appeal to Alan and Arlene. From the beginning, they made a conscious choice to raise their children together. Even today, Alan says, Arlene still has her doubts about day-care centers for preschoolers. No one can convince her that hired professionals can replace a mother's presence during the first two years of a baby's life.

For the first fifteen years of their marriage, Alan and Arlene did raise their children together. Occasionally he'd go out of town for a few weeks to make a movie or try out a new Broadway play, but basically Alan was there—no more of an absentee father than most businessmen with their semiannual conventions and out-of-town sales conferences. But in 1972, $M*A*S*H$ changed all that. Suddenly Alan's work was in California, while his wife and daughters were back east. The Aldas now found themselves apart as much as they were together, shelling out more money to the airline companies each month than most couples pay in rent—and the dollar signs didn't even begin to tell the whole story of the emotional wrench. Alan and Arlene were now caught up in a web of crossed telephone wires, weekend reunions and Sunday-night goodbyes. They were living out an often exasperating arrangement that Hollywood gossip columnists dubiously call "long-distance marriage."

13

In 1972, Alan bridled at the thought of locking himself into a long-running contract with *M*A*S*H*. He dreaded that the move to Hollywood might disrupt his family. Almost thirty years before, his father had faced exactly the same situation when Warner Brothers had offered him the lead in *Rhapsody in Blue*. In his case, there had been no alternative—a husband's work simply came first—and Joan and Alan had packed their bags unquestioningly to follow him out to a new life in California.

Alan's commitment to his wife and daughters weighed so heavily on his mind that he nearly bypassed the chance of a lifetime, in order not to uproot them. When Alan got the go-ahead from 20th Century–Fox and knew that studio lawyers were already drawing up his contract, he phoned Arlene from his Los Angeles hotel, asking her if he should pull out of the project. Alan hated the idea of giving up his home in Leonia, deserting friends, pulling his daughters out of school, and forcing his wife to make a new life for herself in California, which they both considered a cultural wasteland compared to the sophisticated

East. In Alan's mind, moving to Los Angeles—even to star on a promising television series—was like being sentenced to Siberia. The only thing missing was snow.

But Arlene knew her husband—and show business—well enough to realize that *M*A*S*H* was the kind of perfectly timed opportunity that might only come once in an actor's lifetime, and that deep down inside Alan really wanted this role. She also had enough faith in their marriage to believe that she and Alan could survive anything. So while Alan vented all his ifs, buts, and maybes on the phone from L.A. that night, she listened, then told him to stop worrying and sign the contract. They'd lived through his years of unemployment, they'd survived the early religious differences that had nearly made getting married impossible, they'd been separated by the Army, by out-of-town tryouts, by Alan's erratic movie career; they'd survive this too. Somehow, she told him, they'd find a way to bend geography a little, if CBS, Mr. A.C. Nielsen & Company, and all the Fates granted *M*A*S*H* a rich and healthy longevity.

The Los Angeles–Leonia compromise that Alan and Arlene eventually worked out was rather unusual in show business. They managed to live apart for a sizable portion of the year—separated only in the physical sense, never emotionally. Like the goddess Demeter in Greek mythology, Arlene learned to share her loved one with another claimant on his life and time. Six months every year, while *M*A*S*H* was in production, Alan lived in L.A. alone, commuting home to Leonia as frequently as he could. The rest of the year, while the *M*A*S*H* set went dark, Alan was back in the New Jersey suburbs, a full-time parent to his three daughters and a full-time husband to his wife. Just as the Greek myth records that the earth blossomed whenever Demeter's daughter Persephone returned to her, Alan's six months at home was definitely the sunshine of his year. His six months in Hollywood—a married man temporarily suspended into a lonely state of bachelorhood—was like Persephone's semiannual hibernation in the underworld.

Working on *M*A*S*H*, Alan always seemed in a perpetual state of jet lag—a little groggy from sleepless plane rides, a little anxious because so many family problems had to be settled by phone, and never quite sure whether he was operating on Pacific or Eastern Standard Time. At first, he tried flying home only on alternate weekends, but two-week intervals just became too much of a private hell for him to endure without seeing Arlene and the girls. After a few seasons on *M*A*S*H*, as he became wealthy enough to afford it, he started flying home every single weekend during the fall and winter. Every Friday, as soon as he finished shooting, Alan would catch the late-night "red-eye" flight out of Los Angeles airport, arriving at Newark Airport at 6:00 A.M. He'd get home just in time to have breakfast with his family, then nap for the rest of the morning, since he was rarely able to sleep on planes. After spending Saturday and Sunday with Arlene and his daughters, he'd repeat the same routine Sunday night, although the three hours time he gained on the flight back helped ease his sleeping pattern a little.

Alan wasn't the only Hollywood star living apart from his family—the difference was that in his case, it didn't become an excuse to create a new life apart from them. Career separations are usually the prime cause of actors' marriage breakups—since the temptation is great and the loneliness almost overwhelming, and all kinds of girls, from starlets to groupies, are available. Most long-distance marriages usually end in divorce after a year or two because, more often than not, absence makes the heart go wander, but Alan and Arlene Alda managed to "bend geography a little" for seven years without even fender-denting their marriage. If anything, their marriage was stronger than ever by the time their youngest daughter, Beatrice, entered college and Arlene was suddenly free to accompany Alan to California on a regular basis.

Marlo Thomas, who became a close friend of the Aldas when she worked with Alan on *Jenny* in 1970, marveled at the couple's unique arrangement and felt they'd performed a genuine public service by showing ordinary Americans that career vs. family doesn't have to be an unsolvable conflict. Alan's career, as an actor, was in Hollywood. Arlene's career, not just as a homemaker but eventually as a photographer, was in New Jersey. His daughters' lives—tied up with school, friends, and an intricate network of teenage involvements—were also on the East Coast. So the Alda family had decided in very democratic fashion—four to one—that Leonia would still be home and Los Angeles would just be Daddy's home away from home. "The Aldas didn't give up their life-style for Alan's career," Marlo told writer Susan Edmiston. "They're committed more to what's good for them as a family than what's good for his work."

Arlene and Alan had weighed all the pros and cons of moving to California, and the cons had won out.

Alan hated the idea of plunking his kids down in the unchartered labyrinths of the San Fernando Valley or Beverly Hills. To him, Los Angeles was something out of Pinocchio's Candyland—a rich, self-indulgent city without a moral or cultural center. By the early 1970s, the Los Angeles schools were already famous for the prevalence of drugs, for kids who were glazed, crazed and dazed and were far more knowledgeable about cocaine and karma than how to pass a college-entrance exam. Alan was sure of one thing—his kids were getting a good education in Leonia. Their friends were the children of neighbors he liked and respected, who shared a common bond of family and community concerns with him. Why trade that quieter, untrampled paradise for a world where his daughters would associate with kids who traveled only in air-conditioned limousines, whose parents might be top studio executives, producers and stars but who treated their children exactly as they treated their swimming pools, Japanese gardens and Alfa Romeos—something to be cast off into the care of hired help?

Alan's dislike of California was probably a reaction to his own childhood. The years he'd spent in the lush San Fernando Valley had been far from happy. He'd been stricken with polio, isolated from other children. All his close friesdships, and many of his happiest memories, had come later, in the East. In interviews, of course, Alan preferred not to dwell on the past and generally had a flip answer ready and waiting when questioned about his cross-country commuting life. In February 1973, six months after starting on *M*A*S*H*, he blamed the climate on his refusal to uproot his family and joked with columnist Sidney Skolsky, "There's a definite lack of weather here. I don't like to drive to the snow, I like it to come to me, and I hate palm trees and what they stand for." Otherwise, Alan said, California was rather nice.

Later, Alan explained to Robert Berkvist of the *New York Times* that he didn't understand the language people spoke in California. He didn't want to live in a town that measured you only by your latest Nielsen rating. Being a television personality made it difficult enough, Alan said, to maintain any sense of privacy and perspective in your life. He preferred staying in a small town like Leonia where neighbors respected your privacy and refused to turn you into a local landmark. In Leonia, Alan could run into friends in the supermarket and discuss school-bond issues, not ratings and residuals.

Uprooting the family and moving to California would have been an added and, in view of past history, tremendously unfair strain on Arlene.

As a newlywed, Arlene had thought that giving up her seat with a symphony orchestra wouldn't mean abandoning her pursuit of music. While an attorney might need a court of law to practice in and an actor is useless without a stage, a musician, after all, can remain faithful to her art anywhere and derive the same pleasure from playing whether she's on a concert stage or performing in the living room of her own home. But once the babies started coming along, as they did so rapidly, Arlene discovered that laundry, diapering, cooking and tending cranky infants at all hours of the day and night left almost no time for playing the clarinet. Concert music is a demanding business, much like ballet—it's an art that requires constant daily practice in order to keep in shape, not something that a harried young homemaker can steal a few moments for occasionally while the baby's sleeping and the roast is in the oven.

So eventually Arlene put her clarinet aside in favor of household demands. But when her youngest daughter, Beatrice, entered kindergarten, suddenly she had three hours of peace and freedom every day after years of being constantly tied to her children's schedule. To fill up her time, Arlene decided to take an adult education course, and after browsing through the catalog, opted for photography, although it was a toss-up between that and embroidery. Her flair for visual things was quickly apparent to her instructor, and by the end of the course Arlene's photos were good enough for professional appraisal. In the ensuing years, she accepted assignments whenever she could weave them into the family schedule; occasionally she even photographed Alan for top women's magazines like *Good Housekeeping*, and Arlene's pictures would accompany the staff writer's interview pieces on him.

In 1971, not long before Alan landed on *M*A*S*H*, Arlene landed a plum assignment of her own—shooting the jacket photo of author Robert Ludlum for his first novel, *The Scarlatti Inheritance*. Her photo contacts were all in New York and New Jersey, and since Arlene had already given up one promising career—concert music—at the time of their marriage, Alan felt it would be unfair to ask her to make the same sacrifice again.

But as the girls grew older, Arlene reexpanded her horizons, picking up her long-shelved musical career. She organized a chamber-music group in her local area and also began doing some commuting of her own—to Connecticut, where she became clarinetist with a small symphony orchestra. By the time Alan was enjoying his own success on *M*A*S*H*, Arlene had two active careers of her own—photography and music—and both of them could take comfort from the fact that they'd managed to work out their lives in such a way that they could feel artistically satisfied.

Unlike Alan's mother, Arlene has never felt overshadowed or threatened by her husband's ambitions; but on the other hand she's never been diminished by Alan's career, either. She keeps a quiet profile because quietness is an integral part of her nature, not because she fears the limelight or because Alan particularly wants a wife who retreats into the background. According to friends and neighbors, Arlene Alda would go about her life exactly as she does now even if her husband were simply a clerk or a businessman. Feigned elegance has never been and probably never will be her style. She doesn't dress in designer fashions or spend inordinate amounts of money on jewels, furs and other trappings, although the Aldas' multimillion-dollar income could certainly afford it. She's always chosen to cut her hair, rather than style it, because sitting in a beauty salon bores her. The Aldas traditionally have given one party every year for their friends in Leonia. While the guests play tennis—just as filmland aristocrats do at Bel-Air parties—the menu always is and probably always will be barbecued chicken and grilled hamburgers.

Actually, Alan's the extravagant one in the family—and the true romantic at heart. On one birthday, he surprised Arlene by hiring a string quartet to entertain at home; another year he gave a birthday brunch, and dessert turned out to be a trip to Paris. One of the guests, a local businessman, showed up at the party with suitcases in tow, announcing he was leaving on a business trip right afterward. Actually, the suitcases contained all of Arlene's clothes (Alan didn't know what to pack, so he'd packed nearly everything), and after the party when Arlene and Alan drove their friend to the airport, he kept the ruse up till nearly boarding time. Then Alan pulled out the two airplane tickets to Paris—for Arlene and himself.

What strikes interviewers most about Arlene is her complete lack of Hollywood-style glamour. Two years older than Alan, at forty-seven, she's the kind of woman about whom people would simply say, "My, doesn't she look good for her age." "Straightforward," "down-to-earth," "motherly" and "maternal" are the words that reporters recurringly lean on to describe this unique un-Hollywood wife. Her dark eyes flash with warmth and intelligence (but hardly a trace of mascara), and she strikes people as short because her six-foot-two husband towers a full head above her. Cliff Jahr of *Ladies' Home Journal* recently remarked,

"Arlene Alda is not the glamorous type one imagines sex symbols marry—even a gentle sex symbol like Alan." But he added that her quiet charm and sharp mind made her "the perfect counterpoint for her celebrated husband." Judy Klemesrud of the *New York Times* couldn't help noticing that when Arlene showed up to be interviewed she was wearing a simple, subdued dress-and-blazer outfit and "sensible shoes" that "gave her the look of a suburban matron," not a millionaire movie idol's wife.

For the first nine years Alan was on *M*A*S*H*, Arlene didn't meet interviewers at all, with or without her sensible shoes on. In fact, Alan's family kept such a low profile on the publicity scene that few people in Hollywood, beyond the Aldas' close circle of friends, even knew what Arlene or the Alda daughters looked like. This year, however, Arlene finally emerged from her shell, tentatively, to help promote *On Set*, the hardcover photo book she put together of production life on *The Four Seasons*. For the sake of her own career, Arlene agreed to do joint magazine interviews with her husband and even braved the public-appearance circuit alone, promoting her book around the country.

Through the years, Alan and Arlene have maintained the same cool attitude toward his stardom, accepting the hoopla and the hype as a necessary part of his career, yet coexisting with it rather uneasily. The Aldas' judgment on fame has never changed. They treat it exactly the way someone might treat a pesky housefly. It's certainly not the kind of guest you welcome into your home with open arms, but after a while it's not worth the effort to swat. So it's an irritant you learn to live with. Alan used to tell the press that he and Arlene felt that public attention was like weeds creeping up on your front lawn—you just try to keep them from taking over.

So, all through the 1970s, while Alan's stardom demanded that he manufacture glib copy for all the women's magazines, and jest on talk shows occasionally, and sign autographs (even when emerging from the men's room in a restaurant), Arlene preferred to go her own quiet way. She raised their daughters, tended the house, and followed her own interests—music and photography. Her pictures appeared in *Vogue, People, Saturday Evening Post* and *New York* magazine. Along the way, her photos often cropped up on display at various art exhibitions, too.

When Alan was in Baltimore filming *Joe Tynan*, Arlene landed a photo assignment that sent her to India and Nepal. At first, she was leery of leaving the girls alone in New Jersey, but since their youngest daughter was seventeen at the time, Alan felt Arlene was being overcautious. Perhaps Alan remembered his mother's fearful unwillingness to travel without him when he was a teenager; perhaps he thought Arlene, who'd sacrificed so much on his behalf, deserved this opportunity; perhaps his reaction was a little bit of both. At any rate, he knew his daughters were old enough to take care of themselves for a few weeks. Since Alan couldn't delay going to work on *Joe Tynan*, he became a long-distance parent-in-charge while Arlene was in the Far East. Alan would phone home every night to check on the girls, and fly back to Leonia two or three times a week during filming, just to have dinner with them. Those flights were even harder on Alan than his weekly commutes from Los Angeles to New Jersey, since he was rushing to the airport at 5:00 A.M. every other day. But he felt it was a rare chance to give both his wife and his daughters the independence they all deserved.

It also gave Alan a chance to prove he was more than just a lecture-circuit feminist—and even if he spent most of his house-husband stint traveling in airplanes, he certainly made an earnest attempt. Unquestionably, some of Alan's feminism stems from his boyhood, when he felt that sensitivity, not brawniness, was the true mark of a man. Arlene, who undoubtedly knows him better than anyone else, thinks that Alan's concern for women's rights just naturally evolved from the fact that he was always a fair-minded person. She herself was involved in the Women's Strike for Peace, and Alan was searching for a cause of his own to become deeply involved with. He felt his stardom put him in a unique position to make people aware of social injustice, and it would be immoral not to use his fame to promote some kind of social change. Perhaps the fact that he had three daughters made women's rights a particularly appealing cause to him. After all, he wanted to make sure his daughters wouldn't be hampered by sexism when they entered the adult world.

At home, Alan pitches in with some of the everyday chores, although he'd much rather escape to his typewriter and work on a new movie script than clear the table or try his hand at mending. When the girls were infants and he was mainly an unemployed Broadway actor, Alan did share a considerable amount of the parenting—bathing the girls, diapering them, and even rinsing out the diapers. Today, of course, the Aldas can afford hired help to relieve them both of some of the tedious aspects of housework, but Alan still enjoys taking over in the kitchen occasionally. Whenever the family enjoys an Italian-style dinner, Alan cooks the pasta himself, using recipes that he learned from his father and stepmother, who are both skillful cooks. It's an Alda tradition, in fact, that the man of the family double as chef; and Alan's half brother Antony, who's now married, also does pasta duty in his kitchen. When Robert, Flora, Antony and his wife Lori get together with Alan and his family for Christmas and Thanksgiving dinners, the men take over the kitchen completely, leaving the women to chat over drinks in the living room. Alan used that bit of family tradition in the opening scene of *The Four Seasons,* where the three husbands in the movie prepared a gourmet feast while their wives chatted about their careers in another room.

Once Alan took full charge of the household for a month, so Arlene could work on a photographic project. Since *M*A*S*H* was on hiatus, he was home anyway; and Alan was sure that handling one kitchen, one washer, one dryer and three teenage daughters would be a snap. He was in for a rude awakening. With four people in the house, the laundry never stopped—and the cooking was worse. Alan would sift through Julia Child cookbooks, then spend all morning shopping for the right ingredients to make a gourmet feast. He'd spend half the afternoon toiling over the stove, only to be told at the last minute that his daughters wouldn't be home for dinner. After the first day, he was tempted to buy TV dinners and let everyone fend for herself. He stuck it out for the month, but by the time Arlene returned to her role as mistress of the house, Alan was only too happy to hand over the apron strings. His month in the trenches had been more of an education than all his years on the ERA lecture circuit.

The house where all this experimental domesticity takes place is located in Leonia, N.J., a small suburban town that Alan claims is only fifteen minutes from Manhattan (but less courageous drivers usually make the trip in half an hour). Leonia is a sleepy little community of nine thousand people, and the Aldas discovered it in 1964, when Alan was doing summer stock in Paramus. The house is fifty years old, made of frame and painted a nondescript brown. It sits on an ordinary street in Leonia in an area that's far from status-conscious. People still mow their lawns instead of manicuring them, and grass sprouts up between cracks in the aging sidewalk. Broadway lyricist Sheldon Harnick is perhaps the only visitor who ever tried to fashion poetry out of the Alda abode. In 1966, when he was writing the score for *The Apple Tree*, he created a tongue-in-cheek song for Alan Alda as Sanjar, the barbaric gladiator. In the song, Sanjar dreamed of escaping to Gaul with his lady love Barbarra (Barbara Harris) and crooned to her about all the suburban comforts they'd find in their Teutonic paradise, including "a house painted brown/ on the outskirts of town . . . no more feathers and fuss/ just the children and us."

"Feathers and fuss" is certainly not the life-style of Leonia; ultimate middle class is probably a more apt description. In fact, one reporter who captured Alan in his native habitat quipped that in order to become a resident of Leonia, you probably had to be a near-perfect insurance risk.

For nearly eighteen years, Leonia has been home to the Aldas, and from the beginning, Alan and Arlene immersed themselves in community life. Unlike his parents, who were reserved and isolated during their suburban stay in Elmsford, N.Y., Alan and his wife never viewed their town as a place to retreat into themselves and close out the world. They became active in town politics, made enduring friendships among their neighbors, mixed and mingled in supermarkets, at school meetings and local parties. Almost none of their Leonia friends were in show business, which suited Arlene and Alan just fine. They felt very comfortable among "regular people"; in fact a great deal more comfortable than they did around flamboyant Hollywood types.

The Aldas didn't buy their Bel-Air house until 1975, when Alan for the first time had to stop commuting home from California for a long stretch. He'd written a pilot for a new sitcom series called *We'll Get By*, and CBS agreed to air it as a midseason replacement show. So instead of coming home to Leonia after *M*A*S*H* finished up, Alan had to stay in California to write thirteen episodes of *We'll Get By*. Trying to work and live in a hotel—even a posh Beverly Hills hotel—seemed ridiculous, so Arlene flew out to L.A. to help Alan purchase an affordable bachelor pad in Bel-Air (the house cost under half a million dollars; cheap in Los Angeles real estate terms). For the next few years, the Bel Air cottage became his home away from home.

Once the girls were all off in college, however, Alan's bi-coastal commuting life ended. With Arlene joining him in L.A. during the six months that he filmed *M*A*S*H*, their piece of West Coast property suddenly seemed a wise investment. Today, the Aldas spend only half the year in Leonia and half the year in the compact three-bedroom cottage in Bel-Air, one of L.A.'s trendiest star-studded communities. Their posh southern California address, however, is still their only concession to success. In Bel-Air, Alan and Arlene share the housework and employ only a gardener to tend the lawn. For summers back on the East Coast, they're also building a Long Island beach house on a 53-acre parcel of land they recently bought.

Whether ensconced in Bel-Air or Leonia, the Aldas live quietly. They play scrabble and chess, listen to baroque music and read to each other. When Alan's browsing through the evening newspaper, he's constantly reporting what he reads to Arlene, since they both like to discuss political issues. He gets up at 6:30 A.M. to play tennis, goes shopping with Arlene for oil paintings at Sotheby Parke Bernet, and enjoys cooking Chinese dinners, Szechwan-style. Arlene divides her time between piano lessons (she started taking them a few years ago just for fun) and working on her next photographic project (a children's alphabet book with pictures of orginary things like seesaws and kitchen utensils to illustrate the letters).

Amazingly, despite the fact that Arlene is an accomplished photographer herself, she's very camera-shy when it's her turn to pose. All three daughters have followed her lead, and pictures of the Alda family are rarely taken in public. Not long ago, Alan—in a rare display of public fury—became enraged when Hollywood photographer Ron Gallela accidentally stepped on his daughter's foot trying to snap the family on a night out. Run-ins with photographers are rare, however, because over the years Alan has developed a nearly foolproof method for shielding his family from the cameras. When they leave a theater or concert, Arlene and the girls usually slip out of a side door, while Alan faces photographers alone at the front entrance.

Alan has insisted on keeping his daughters out of the spotlight as zealously as other parents impose a dating curfew or worry about their kids' sampling marijuana, though those more mundane concerns affect him, too. His antagonism toward notoriety isn't just overprotectiveness on his part—it comes straight from his own childhood and the feelings that his father's fame gave him. "I grew up the son of a famous man," Alan says, "and it wasn't an easy burden for a kid to bear." Alan remembers dining with his father in Hollywood restaurants and feeling that they might as well have been on display. Alan would be trying to tell his father about something really important to him when a reporter would come over to their table and interrupt. At times, Alan felt he was competing with the whole world for his father's attention. More than once, Alan and Robert would be walking down the street, enjoying a private conversation, when an aggressive fan would run up to them, begging for an autograph, making inane remarks and completely disrupting their peaceful afternoon. Once, in fact, a "fan" who apparently hadn't liked Robert Alda's latest film had actually accosted him on the street and slapped his face, while Alan shriveled up in terror.

Those kinds of bizarre experiences, which unfortunately beset every well-known actor from time to time—are just what Alan wants to shield his own daughters from.

14

Curiously enough, the childhood experiences engendered by his being a celebrity's son never made Alan detest show business itself—far from it; he couldn't wait to finish up at Fordham and get his own acting career going. But it did leave him permanently repelled by the rootlessness of the life. In a sense, his stoic commitment to family first has turned Alan into an anti-star. In years past, that label has been applied to rebellious actors like James Dean and Marlon Brando who bucked the Hollywood system, defying studios, producers and all the old rules of Hollywood protocol. They were anti-stars, individualists who refused to buckle under and let the studios manipulate their careers. But they were anti-stars only in a professional sense. In their tortured personal lives, their wrecked relationships, flamboyant behavior and uncontainable egos made them stars in the true Hollywood tradition.

Alan Alda, however, is an anti-star of a far more subtle breed. He actually eschews the superstar lifestyle, remaining zealously middle-class in a working environment that freely offers every variety of hedo-

171

nistic pleasure possible. Alan is like the bearded medieval Jewish merchant entering the gates of Rome to sell his wares, doing business with the Christians, bartering with them in their own language, yet remaining permanently a wary stranger among them, faithful to his own customs and his own God.

What could be more the true mark of an anti-star than Alan's recurring remarks on his own prejudice against the swinging-singles world? He openly admits he chooses friends who value family life—and whether by coincidence or planning, almost every single long-running castmate on *M*A*S*H* has a spotless marriage record that equals his own. "I'm at a loss for conversation with men who are swinging bachelors," Alan says. "I don't speak their language, and they don't speak mine." And for a man who feels comfortable discussing anything from astronomy to Zoroastrianism, it's rather remarkable that Alan can't find anything to say to people who don't have children—or at least care about them. But he confesses it's true. "If somebody I meet isn't interested in relationships, in family, in parents and kids, I lapse into silence very quickly."

The only other subject that, for Alan, is a sure conversation killer is sports. He's never followed baseball or football and wouldn't know the KC Royals from the NY Jets—or particularly care which was which. Alan prefers to talk about ideas, issues and people; and to his mind, sports talk is a superficial kind of gab between men. Similarly, he also views much of the glamour life of an actor as superficial, too.

Many times in his career, work has made separation unavoidable. In 1961, when Arlene was pregnant with their youngest daughter, Beatrice, Alan had to be away from home for two and a half months; and for the first time in their marriage, Arlene wasn't able to go with him. Before he left, Alan figured he'd be able to get back to New York every weekend, but it turned out to be impossible—and the weeks apart were agonizing for both Alan and Arlene. Sensibly, they realized then that they'd just have to make a conscious effort to learn to live with separations—to rely on trust and love and commitment—or distance would breed jealousy and discontent. Over the years, long before he arrived on *M*A*S*H*, Alan was frequently away from home, going to Boston and Philadelphia and New Haven for pre-Broadway tryouts, going on location to make *Paper Lion* and *Jenny*. The fact that Alan and Arlene survived those separations turned out to be excellent preparation for *M*A*S*H* and the coast-to-coast commuting that became a regular part of their lives.

So much of their time has actually been spent apart that Alan and Arlene leap at any excuse to tear up their schedules and be together. A heartwarming case in point is May 1974, when Alan won his first Emmy for *M*A*S*H*. Arlene was back in New Jersey when Alan got an early tip-off on the set of *M*A*S*H* that he'd won, and as soon as the show wrapped up for the day, he rushed to his hotel room to phone Arlene with the good news. When he called, it was evening in Leonia and Arlene had turned the answering machine on. So Alan simply shouted his news into the machine. Later that night, Arlene listened to the message and instantly decided she had to fly to L.A. to be with her husband for the Emmy ceremonies.

In order to accomplish that, she had to move heaven and earth, finding someone trustworthy to stay with the girls, finding mothers to take over her car-pool assignments, making plane reservations and rearranging her own commitments to photography and her chamber-music group. And she had only a few hours to tie up all the loose ends, pack and deposit herself at the airport. But the next morning, Arlene landed in L.A. and showed up at 20th Century—Fox just as the $M*A*S*H$ battalion was filing out of the studio for lunch. The look of genuine joy on Alan's face—and the unabashed warmth with which he greeted her—made his Emmy victory seem pale by comparison.

Also because of the frequent separations, Alan and Arlene had to make a conscious effort to learn to be independent of each other. Otherwise, the loneliness would have been intolerable. Arlene pursued her own interests while her husband was away. During his long stretches alone in California, Alan turned back to his first love, writing, to fill up his free time. At first, he wrote episodes of $M*A*S*H$, then pilots for other TV ventures, and eventually screenplays for movies.

To the world at large, that knew the Aldas only from reading about them in the women's magazines, this marriage seemed remarkable indeed. And pretty soon, Alan began getting letters from fans who idolized him not so much because he was a talented actor or a sexy man, but simply because he was a caring husband—a very rare type in American life these days. In letters, women poured out their admiration for him and the grief of their own lives. They wished their husbands could be as considerate and understanding; they also wished they could blend work and family as magically as the Aldas did. Letters like these touched Alan deeply, but also frightened him at the same time. Suddenly, he and Arlene were being held up to America as a "super couple," when all they really wanted to do was be left alone to go about their own business. But like it or not, Alan Alda was suddenly a role model for a new breed of husband—sensitive, concerned, liberated, secure enough to let his wife carve out her own path instead of following dutifully behind him.

Alan lists mutual respect and encouragement as the real secret of their happy marriage. He's not so sure whether they're a "super couple" or not, but when problems arise, they do take turns being the tower of strength. At times, Arlene will help Alan through a crisis, listening to his complaints, guiding him to find a solution. And when the situation is reversed, Alan will do the same for her. There is nothing that happens in either of their lives that they can't discuss.

And the discussions don't always take place in the privacy of their own home. When Alan and Arlene attend dinner parties, they very often spend most of the evening talking to each other. The only time silence intrudes is when Alan's writing at home. Then practically nothing can interfere with his concentration. When he first started writing and retreating into himself, Arlene would become tense and moody as a result. But gradually they both learned to adjust. And because Alan respects his wife's judgment so much, he now uses her as a critic for what comes out of the typewriter. Alan always shows her the first draft, and Arlene very candidly tells him whether she thinks the plot and dialogue are plausible or not.

In many ways, the Aldas give the impression of being such serious-minded and conscientious individuals—listening to chamber music, discussing ideas and philosophy, devouring artistic projects as other couples devour pizza—that the public does not focus on their warmth and earthiness. Alan, for all his outgoing qualities, is not a man who jokes or banters about intimate things, especially the intimate details of his life. Occasionally, though, his guard accidentally slips a little and he reveals something he probably never intended to. A case in point is the unusual bed scene he wrote for *The Seduction of Joe Tynan*. The script called for Alan and Meryl Streep, who played his uninhibited mistress, to laugh while they made love, teasing and tickling each other like two kids having a pillow fight.

Alan thought the scene was sensual—and realistic. Director Jerry Schatzberg thought the laughter destroyed the sensuality because, as he told Alan, people just didn't do things like that in the heat of passion. Alan insisted they did, and the scene stayed; in fact, it became one of the most effective moments in the movie, blending playfulness with erotica. Later, Alan blushed when reporters asked him if the scene was inspired by his own marital experience. But Arlene, who's apparently more comfortable discussing such things, admitted that she and Alan regularly tickle each other under the covers.

Perhaps Arlene's less reticent because she's the more practical of the two. Arlene calls herself cynical at times—"realistic" might be the better word—but Alan's definitely the romantic. While he'd never talk about sex in an interview, he rhapsodizes about love at length, in a poetic, chivalrous way.

There's no doubt about it, Alan Alda looks at women and love like Don Quixote, not Dr. Kinsey. And the only thing he's firm about is that love isn't a passing intoxication, it's a relationship that stands the test of time. He says that love "isn't your heart beating faster when you look at someone walk by while you're sitting at a Paris café," but "your heart beating faster when you realize all over again how much you love someone who's been with you for years."

In *The Four Seasons*, Alan the screenwriter declares that "love comes in waves." You go through periods in a marriage where you're barely aware of the other person, at times simply can't stand them, but every once is a while you fall head over heels in love with that person all over again. And each time love returns, that wave of intensity is so tremendous it makes all the other times of doubt and drifting and compromise worthwhile.

15

Cecil Smith, a reporter for the *Los Angeles Times*, once remarked that Alan Alda was "raising his kids out of the show biz mainstream much as if he were an accountant from Scranton."

The girls were not quite in their teens when *M*A*S*H* turned their father from an ordinary actor into a major television personality, but success never changed the ground rules at home. Eve, Elizabeth and Beatrice were all brought up to be thoughtful and responsible human beings. The incredible sums of money their father earned hardly touched them at all, and they still had to argue like the dickens to get their allowance upped or their curfews extended. Alan may have changed his tax bracket and the kind of car he drove when he became a Hollywood star, but he remained a middle-class suburban parent at heart. Like most parents, he tried to walk the tightrope between love and discipline; apparently, he did a very successful job.

Today, all three girls are strong and independent, close to their parents without being umbilically tied to the nest. All three are brown-haired and brown-eyed—a pleasant combination of their father's Italian ancestry and their mother's Eastern European Jewish background. Eve, at twenty-two, lives in Boston, where she works as a psychologist. When she was seventeen, she spent her first summer in Europe alone; and while she has no interest in show business, she's the most politically active of the girls and has often joined her father on the platform at local political rallies. Elizabeth, who's known around the house as Liz, is a twenty-year-old junior at Kenyon College in Ohio. She's the quietest member of the bunch, a contemplative soul like her father and a talented musician like her mother. Beatrice, who's nineteen, attends college in Connecticut. She's the social dynamo and the only sports fiend in the family. In fact, it was Beatrice who got Alan to start attending school games when she started signing up for teams at the age of thirteen.

The girls have turned out so well that Alan jokes that he and Arlene have earned a graduation certificate from the American College of Parents. Although he recently allowed Liz and Beatrice to appear in cameo roles in *The Four Seasons*, there was no fatherly coercion involved. He agreed to turning the movie into a family affair only because he felt the girls were finally old enough to handle the glamour and the pressure—and because they both wanted the opportunity so much. Alan is a firm believer in guiding children, not molding them. "Don't make demands on your kids that you wouldn't make on other people," he's often said; and if it sounds a bit like the Golden Rule, it's a rule that Alan and Arlene have faithfully followed. Discussing, disagreeing and negotiating were things the girls were always encouraged to do at home. Alan and Arlene remained the final judges, but decisions were reached only after the girls got a fair hearing.

Summer jobs were always a must. While studying psychology at the University of Connecticut, Eve worked as a volunteer at Boston's Children's Hospital. Liz wasn't allowed to spend her vacations just hanging around the house, either; and when Beatrice was a high school senior, she spent her summer on the set of M*A*S*H, running errands and fielding phone calls for her father—Alan had hired her as his personal secretary.

The girls all attended private high school in New Jersey; and although the Aldas were wealthier than most of the other parents, luxuries had to be earned, not simply demanded. Eve and her sisters were among the few seniors who didn't automatically get cars as graduation gifts. They started getting small allowances from the time they were in grade school, but only if their assigned chores around the house got done on time. Alan and Arlene gave each of the girls a clothes budget, but anything frivolous had to be saved for.

According to Liz, Alan was a lot freer with money than Arlene, and in a financial crunch she and her sisters would generally run to him. Since he was in California so much, he got into the habit of opening his wallet anytime he was hit for a loan, the minute he came home to Leonia. But Arlene eventually put her foot down, and she and Alan developed a united front on the issue of spending money. On almost everything else, they agreed. Of course, Arlene was home a lot more than her husband and did most of the hassling with the girls over everyday things.

All through the '70s—despite Alan's stardom and Arlene's life as a musician and photographer—the Aldas made it a point to stay in touch with their daughters' school lives. At least one parent was there to represent the family on open school night, and homework assignments and report cards were carefully checked. On the whole, the girls never suffered because of their famous father. Since they stayed well out of the limelight, their classmates were only casually aware of the Hollywood connection. Every once in a while, though, Alan would fume over a teacher who was judging his daughter—for better or worse—not on the basis of her own abilities, but on the fact that she was Alan Alda's daughter. "No matter now much you try to shield them, TV stardom remains tough on your children," Alan has often said.

When Alan was growing up, his own famous father had taken a more casual attitude about exposing his son to the limelight. Alan was allowed to wander around burlesque theaters in New York, and later to perform onstage with his father at the Hollywood Canteen. In raising his own children, Alan became far more puritanical—and even though Liz and Beatrice were drawn to acting from an early age, he kept them well removed from the Hollywood scene. Indeed, as far as the girls were concerned, he might just as well have been an accountant from Scranton.

But an interesting problem arose in 1975 when Alan wrote the pilot for the CBS comedy series *We'll Get By*. The point of the show, as expressed in the theme song, was "learning to be a family isn't easy," and the trials and tribulations of the Platts and their three children were definitely modeled after Alan's own clan. The most compelling character was Andrea Platt, a bright, sensitive, slightly gawky adolescent who painfully alternated between stoic maturity and stubborn childishness. Andrea Platt was modeled directly on Alan's own daughter Eve, who was sixteen at the time.

Eve had never shown any interest in acting, so Alan didn't even consider casting her for the role. An open audition was held, in which dozens of experienced teenage actresses tested for the part; and the producers' first choice was Devon Scott (who happened to be George C. Scott's daughter). But even though Devon's performance had been nothing short of brilliant, Alan suddenly felt guilty about giving the part to a stranger. So he convinced CBS not to make a final decision, and went home to talk things over with Eve. He told Eve that he didn't want to encourage her to become an actress against her will, but he also didn't want to be unfair to her. She was, after all, the real Andrea Platt. If Eve wanted, he'd let her do a screen test and then let the producers judge between her performance and Devon's. At first, Eve got excited about trying out, but after viewing Devon Scott's screen test, she changed her mind. With no formal acting training, she realized she could never match, much less outshine, Devon, and she didn't want to put her father in the awkward position of choosing between his own daughter and a very talented young actress. So Devon got the role, as planned.

The Four Seasons, of course, was an entirely different matter. Alan admits he purposely created roles in the film for Liz and Beatrice (as his daughter and Len Cariou's daughter), then gave them the option of accepting or rejecting the assignments. Since he already knew they wanted to become actresses and since they weren't kids anymore he thought it might be a good idea to give them a taste of what moviemaking was all about. That way they could get a feeling for acting in a very controlled environment—with Alan as scriptwriter and director—and decide if show business was what they really wanted. Also, they could never accuse their father of keeping them away from Hollywood because of his rigid feelings about celebrity children. Alan, in a sense, was letting Liz and Beatrice taste show business the way other parents let their offspring sip wine. A small dose of forbidden fruit, with parental approval, might head off an overdose at a later date.

Whether Liz and Beatrice got acting out of their systems by doing *The Four Seasons* or will pursue acting on their own after this remains to be seen. Certainly their film debuts weren't substantial enough to make them feel like overnight stars. They still don't get recognized in airports or restaurants, which Alan feels is all to the good. To him, there's no worse fate that can befall a human being than instant success. Alan equates it with shooting up on heroin—the high is fantastic, but the crash that comes afterward can destroy a person.

Over the years, Alan has become nearly as famous for his success in marriage as for his success on *M*A*S*H* or indeed any of his other professional roles. Newspaper and magazine interviewers devote endless paragraphs to reaffirming the fact that Alan is a very happily married man and to dissecting his intense devotion to family life at length. While Alan shies away from talking about other private areas of his life, marriage is a topic Alan can't seem to discuss enough. "My work outside the home is no more important than my work inside the home," he states repeatedly; and in 1976 *Redbook* reporter Susan Edmiston concluded that Alan Alda is "perhaps the only male celebrity to whom the question traditionally asked female stars—'If it ever came to a choice, which would you give up, your career or your family?'—would be a meaningful one."

Ms. Edmiston believed that in a crunch, Alan would probably find a way not to sacrifice either; and certainly his intense careerism, often played down in the women's magazines in favor of his intense domesticism, is a quality that comes directly from his hard-driving and ambitious father. Yet while everyone notes what a super-success Alan is in the long-running-husband department, no one has ever bothered to explore how much his loyalty to his wife and daughters may be a reaction to his own childhood.

Maybe his formula is as simple as "Don't make the same mistakes your parents did."

Caught in the middle as a young man, Alan witnessed the tortured disintegration of his parents' marriage. If anything, what he saw in his own home, through his parents' struggles, was a warning that simply going through the motions of being married wasn't enough. A partnership between a man and a woman was tricky business, and you had to keep working at it, watching over it, protecting it, day after day, year after year. Some children of divorce become so disillusioned by their parents' failure that they dodge relationships all their lives, afraid to trust another person, afraid to love, because they might get hurt. Alan chose a different, but equally fanatic, route. He approached his own marriage with a dedication—a need to make it work, no matter what—that had all the fervor of a religious crusader.

And to ensure the success of his marriage, he would do things differently than his parents had. Alan grew up in a show-business household, moving from coast to coast, changing schools and addresses whenever his father's career took a new turn. Maybe if the family had had roots somewhere, instead of swinging back and forth between New York and Hollywood, they might have grown closer together over the years instead of farther apart. So, the first thing Alan did was make sure his own family did have roots when he and Arlene purchased the Leonia house. And even when Alan's work on *M*A*S*H* kept him in Los Angeles for six months out of every year, he refused to transplant his family to the West Coast. Alan preferred the strain of commuting back and forth by plane every weekend to the thought of uprooting his wife and daughters, asking them to leave their friends and school and neighbors to accommodate his professional needs. Explaining why the Aldas never left Leonia, his friend and frequent costar Carol Burnett says that Alan saw "no reason to change your life once you're happy."

Perhaps he remembered how many times his father had changed his life. Remembered—and refused to expose his wife and daughters to the same kind of vagabond existence.

In other ways, too, consciously or unconsciously, Alan has not repeated his parents' domestic pattern. An only child himself, with no brothers or sisters to deflect some of the parental heat, Alan, while hardly in a financial position to accommodate a growing family, became the father of three children, in quick succession, by the time he was only twenty-five. And he chose a very different kind of wife than his father had. Arlene pursued her own creative outlets—music and photography—so that motherhood and his career weren't her only reasons for existence. In many ways, like so many women of her generation Alan's mother had been a dependent wife, known to the public only as Mrs. Robert Alda, directly sharing his struggles and setbacks, yet only caught up in his triumphs as a backstage and often lonely observer. In the end, as Alan saw it, the fact that she'd never had a career of her own certainly hadn't helped save the marriage.

Arlene, a Jewish girl with an impatient attitude toward the rigid formality of any religion, was certainly a far cry from Alan's devout Catholic mother. Yet over the years, Alan and Arlene proved closer in spirit than if they'd practiced the same religion, been nurtured in the same ethnic tradition.

Robert Alda was married by the time he was nineteen. Alan took the same step when he was twenty-one. By the standards of any generation, they were both awfully young for such a crucial step.

16

In the spring of 1974, just as he won an Emmy for
M*A*S*H, Alan was basking in the glow of another
television triumph. That March he costarred with
Carol Burnett in the video version of *Six Rms Riv Vu*.
On Broadway Jerry Orbach had teamed with Jane
Alexander in this mild and delightful comedy about a
man and a woman (both married) who meet and
share a brief moment of rapture, while haggling over
the same rent-controlled Manhattan apartment. Bob
Randall, who wrote the play, based the title on the
kind of rental ads that regularly appeared in the *New
York Times*, in this case pointing up the fact that the
apartment had six rooms and a possible view of the
Hudson River.

The apartment was a steal—and so, in a sense, was
Alan's role. After losing the film version of *The Owl
and the Pussycat* to George Segal and watching *The
Apple Tree* never make it to Hollywood at all, Alan
was now turning the tables a bit. His sudden stardom,
thanks to *M*A*S*H*, made him a far more logical
candidate for the TV special than Jerry Orbach, who
was more strictly a New York stage actor. Alan had

first dreamed about playing the lead in *Six Rms Riv Vu* when he caught the play on Broadway in the early '70s, but he was sure the movie roles would go to box-office favorites like Robert Redford and Jane Fonda. However, in an unusual bit of Hollywood bargaining, *Six Rms Riv Vu* was never sold to a movie studio at all. Instead, TV producer Joe Hamilton optioned it as the perfect vehicle for his wife, Carol Burnett. Until then, very few Broadway plays had been sold directly to television—among the notable exceptions were *Dames at Sea*, *The Fantasticks* and Arthur Miller's *The Price*. Economics was probably the reason. In earlier days, TV producers weren't in the habit yet of outbidding movie studios for hot Broadway projects and novels. It would take groundbreaking successes like *Roots* and *Rich Man, Poor Man* to convince television that spending millions on optioning big properties was worth it.

For Carol Burnett, the role was something of a departure. Although she'd already done her first dramatic film, *Pete n' Tillie*, to much acclaim, television audiences had never seen her in a show totally without singing, dancing or slapstick. Carol, however, has an uncanny sixth sense about choosing costars whose styles synchronize completely with hers. Her TV specials with Julie Andrews had been a smash, and her choice of Harvey Korman as her leading man on her own weekly show was possibly one of the finest comedic couplings ever on television. Her choice of Alan Alda for *Six Rms Riv Vu* was equally smart. Not only was Alan's newfound popularity on *M*A*S*H* a built-in ratings draw, but he had the same loose and improvisational style of comedy as Carol.

After phoning Alan to offer him the role, Carol and her husband, Joe Hamilton, invited him to dinner to discuss the TV adaptation. During dinner, Alan got so carried away telling them how he'd stage the play for television if he were in control that Hamilton actually offered him the opportunity to direct as well as star. Since Alan's experience with blocking and camera angles was rather limited at that point, Alan served as creative director on the project, while Hamilton brought in a technical director under him to handle the mechanics of filming.

Hamilton, Burnett and Alda were such a compatible trio that their friendship endured long after *Six Rms Riv Vu* was wrapped up and televised. For years, Alan and Carol talked about doing another project together, but they were constantly committed elsewhere. Still, Alan kept her in mind, and when he wrote *The Four Seasons*, she was his first and only choice to play his wife in the film. Similarly, he'd called upon another old friend, Barbara Harris, to play his wife in *Joe Tynan*. This sort of "closed" casting may or may not be coincidental. In both films, Alan explores very complex marriage relationships between people who've been together a very long time. Choosing actresses he knows, respects and has worked with previously helps create an extra layer of reality in the performances.

After working with him in *Six Rms Riv Vu* and *The Four Seasons*, Carol Burnett had only one gripe. Things went so smoothly with Alan in control, she thought Alan should hire someone to be mean on the set—just to remind everyone they were making a movie, not just partying.

Just after New Year's in 1977, Alan put aside comedy completely to portray Caryl Chessman, the man who spent twelve years on Death Row in San Quentin. During his long imprisonment, Chessman had become a *cause célèbre*—the quintessential rehabilitated criminal—and Alan took on the role as an opportunity to make a strong public statement against capital punishment. The movie, titled *Kill Me If You Can*, aired on NBC.

To prepare for the role, Alan spoke with people who had been intimately connected with the Chessman case. He interviewed two Los Angeles detectives who had been responsible for arresting Chessman in 1948, and he also met with Vince Edwards, who had portrayed Chessman in a 1958 version of his life story. Edwards had actually gone to San Quentin to see Chessman before making the movie, and he was able to offer Alan some incisive clues into the man's personality. For the TV version, Talia Shire was chosen to play Rosalie Asher, Chessman's attorney and close friend; but Miss Asher herself served as a script consultant to help keep the complicated legal facts of the case accurate. Physically, Alan barely resembled Chessman, so the makeup department at the NBC Burbank studios curled his hair, gave him an artifical hook nose and inserted a wire brace inside his mouth to change the shape of his lips.

After eight reprieves, Chessman finally went to the electric chair in 1960—seventeen years before Alan began filming *Kill Me If You Can*. But the project suddenly became very timely, because in the midst of filming, word came that Gary Gilmore had just been executed in Utah. NBC had set up a number of press interviews to generate publicity for *Kill Me If You Can*, and the Gilmore case only intensified Alan's views about capital punishment. He spent most of his time telling journalists that the electric chair (or in Gilmore's case, death by firing squad) was an irrational approach to solving crime, and no deterrent to murder at all. Alan believed then—and still does—that capital punishment only helps generate a "climate of murder" in America and children grow up believing that society condones the taking of one life for another.

But his best weapon for changing people's minds turned out to be the movie itself. After the film aired, newspapers reported that a Florida district attorney dropped out of a public debate where he was scheduled to defend capital punishment. After seeing *Kill Me If You Can*, he no longer favored the death penalty.

Alan had agreed to star in *Kill Me If You Can* because he felt the Caryl Chessman case and its implicit indictment of capital punishment was a worthwhile television venture, a public service that he accepted almost as a matter of conscience. All through the 1970s, Alan could have had his pick of other TV movie roles, but he turned such offers down. Partially, he was stand-offish because he found the scripts insipid and saw no point in simply gaining added TV exposure if the project wasn't up to the quality level of his own show, *M*A*S*H*. But mainly Alan wasn't all that eager to devote himself to acting anymore. For as long as he could remember, Alan had wanted to be a writer, and now *M*A*S*H* had given him both the money and the clout to pursue that dream. It made sense to turn his typewriter in the direction of television first; after all, if he wasn't happy with the quality of most television shows, what better way to change the medium than by sitting down and putting some of his own ideas on paper?

As a child, Alan had written skits to impress his father's Hollywood friends. In high school, inspired by a kind English teacher, he wrote plays for the drama club that did SRO business and made him a star of his graduating class. All through college, Alan wrote sporadically, too; then once his professional acting career began, he let dust gather on his typewriter and for many years didn't think seriously about writing at all.

For one thing, the art of writing takes time—and

191

from 1957 to 1972, time was in short supply in Alan's life. Though in the early years he was an unemployed actor a great deal of the time, he was always working at one temporary job or another in order to make ends meet. Later, when film and Broadway roles began coming his way, he was either in production preparing for a role or doing six evening performances and two matinees a week. What little free time he had belonged to his family. With three small daughters in the house, Alan didn't have much opportunity to shut himself off alone somewhere and draft a play or film script.

In fact, if M*A*S*H hadn't come along, Alan might never have returned to writing. But the long separations from his family that began in 1972, when he moved to California, suddenly gave him the time and isolation that he needed to try his hand at scripting.

During his first season on M*A*S*H, Alan lived in a rented apartment in Beverly Hills. He was too much of a family man to hang out and socialize after the show, and he only went back to Leonia on scattered weekends, so his nights were absolutely free. To fill the time, he began writing in the evenings, at first simply for his own enjoyment, eventually with the idea of turning his scripts into future television projects. Later, when he moved out of the Beverly Hills apartment and into his own house in Bel-Air, his typewriter and growing pile of scripts (mostly half-finished) went with him.

In 1973, Alan almost sold his first original story for television. He presented CBS with an outline for a series about the life of a New York politician. The network expressed cautious enthusiasm, but demanded one crucial change. The New York politician had to become a Midwestern or California politician, because the latest marketing research showed that the average American viewer had a very negative image of New York. To mainstream America, the Big Apple was a decadent, crumbling city inhabited mainly by muggers and welfare recipients. CBS felt a show based on New York politics would be a poor ratings risk.

But Alan, who'd spent most of his life in the New York area, refused to budge on this point. It was a city he knew intimately, and turning his hero from a Manhattan hotshot into a Midwestern nice guy would have destroyed the realism. Besides, Alan felt that the network's anti-New Yorkism was a dangerous prejudice—in the same league with anti-feminism and anti-ethnicism—and he had no wish to cater to it. Rather than compromise his principles, he withdrew the project from network consideration. "I decided it would be better to wait and do it right than do it now and do it wrong," Alan said.

He did wait, and eventually he did do it right. Six years later, that abortive television script was remodeled for the movie screen and became *The Seduction of Joe Tynan*, Alan's first motion-picture screenplay. Although the film was set primarily in Washington, D.C., Joe Tynan was a senator from New York.

But CBS remained impressed with Alan's screenwriting potential, despite the fact that they couldn't come to terms on his first series idea. During long talks with Alan, the discussion veered to one of his favorite topics, the decline of the American family, and CBS encouraged him to come up with an outline for a comedy-drama about a modern American family that would delve into parent-child relationships with a lot of laughs—and a little more punch than *Father Knows Best* had. Those preliminary discussions, which Alan filed away very carefully in his mind, eventually led to *We'll Get By*, the comedy series he wrote that aired briefly in 1975.

Meanwhile, Alan was refining his talents as a story developer and dialogue writer by contributing occasional scripts to his own show, *M*A*S*H*. During the very first season, he wrote a hilarious episode called "The Longjohn Flap," which used a simple comic setup about cold weather and a pair of pajamas to create thirty minutes of farce. In that episode, Hawkeye got a pair of longjohns in the mail, and since it was freezing cold in Korea, everyone from Major Burns to Colonel Blake began hatching secret plots to get their hands on Hawkeye's longjohns. The following season, Alan collaborated with Robert Klane on "Dr. Pierce and Mr. Hyde," an episode chronicling Hawkeye's erratic behavior.

In 1976, Alan contributed an episode called "Dear Sigmund," which was memorable for its stark theme and almost total lack of humor. It centered around a visiting psychiatrist (played by Allan Arbus) who dropped in to check up on the mental health of the *M*A*S*H* unit and gradually lapsed into a severe depression himself. The doctor, unconsolable after being unable to save a young GI, vented his frustrations at the futility and horror of war in a letter to Sigmund Freud, the father of psychiatry. Alan's script was nominated for an Emmy that season, and although he lost in that category, he did win for his direction of that episode.

Although Alan's first two *M*A*S*H* scripts focused on his own character, Hawkeye, the success of "Dear Sigmund" encouraged him to contribute story ideas for the show's other characters. After actor Bill Christopher came down with hepatitis in real life, Alan wrote an episode in which Bill's character, Father Mulcahy, developed the same illness. He also scripted a Radar story in which Hawkeye sent Corporal O'Reilly to a brothel in Seoul, then suffered enormous guilt when Radar was shot down and wounded en route to his one-night stand with a geisha girl. In 1977, Alan also scripted a reprise appearance for Allan Arbus as Major Sidney Freedman. Later, he wrote a romantic interlude for Hawkeye, involving his compassionate attachment to a young Korean widow, and a two-parter in which Hawkeye and Hot Lips briefly became lovers when their jeep broke down on an isolated road. "Dear Sis"—which also had an Alan Alda byline—was the 1978 Christmas show. The episode dealt with the morbid atmosphere that hung over the 4077th as the officers and enlisted men looked forward to another bleak Christmas in their barracks, thousands of miles from their families. And the man most depressed by the holiday season was Father Mulcahy, who confided his secret feelings of anger and frustration in a letter to his sister.

But the episode that stands as Alan's crowning achievement was "Inga," the story of a Swedish surgeon (played by Mariette Hartley). Hawkeye fell under her spell—and she nearly broke down all his romantic defenses—until he saw her in a different light in the M*A*S*H operating room. When she turned out to be a more skillful surgeon than he was, Hawkeye's ardor cooled instantly. The feminist theme of this episode came from a real-life encounter. One night Alan was having dinner with some friends and one of the ladies disagreed with him sharply. Although Alan always prided himself on being able to outargue anyone, her reasoning proved quicker than his, and he was piqued. Later, he realized that despite his intellectual commitment to feminism, he still felt emotionally uncomfortable in a situation where he had to learn something from a woman. Analyzing his own feelings, Alan decided to use that problem as a dilemma for Hawkeye and wrote a script depicting Hawkeye's wounded vanity when Inga tried to teach him a new surgical technique in front of his male *M*A*S*H* colleagues. The script won Alan an Emmy, making him the only major television star to ever win Emmys as an actor, writer and director.

Alan first began directing occasional episodes of *M*A*S*H* in 1974, and over the years he's directed about twenty-five shows, taking over control both creatively and technically. When Alan directs *M*A*S*H*, he rehearses the cast, puts them through their paces on the set and blocks out every scene with them, and when shooting is over, he stays with the show all the way through the final editing process.

After establishing himself as a writer and director on his own series, it was only logical for Alan to want to broaden his horizons a little. And by 1974, he was bound and determined to create and develop an original series for prime time, a show where he would function behind the scenes and turn over the acting reins entirely to other performers. From the time he wrote his first play, Alan wasn't content unless he could be in charge theatrically. On *That Was the Week That Was*, he asserted himself as a group leader among the rest of the cast, although his weekly role was comparatively small. On every movie and TV show he worked on, he did more than just punch in and out as an actor. During rehearsals, he was always contributing ideas and suggesting changes, eager to learn about the technical aspects of production. Unlike so many actors who just come in and learn their lines, Alan had to get involved in everything. For him, the move into creating and writing his own television series was inevitable. It wasn't so much a case of ego as simple restlessness. Alan always had a keen mind and a taste for challenge. His interests were too broad to be confined by a pleasantly successful acting role, even on a hit series like *M*A*S*H*. Just to be Hawkeye Pierce week after week, even if he got to write his own dialogue, choreograph his own camera angles and write his own ticket contractually, wasn't enough to satisfy him.

Alan was mesmerized by all the changes that were happening on prime-time television—and he wanted to be part of it. It was the golden age of situation comedy, and the fact that his own show, *M*A*S*H*, had pioneered so much of the change only impelled him to want to change the state of television even more. Not only were *M*A*S*H*, *All in the Family* and *The Mary Tyler Moore Show* breaking ground—with thoughtful subject matter, ensemble-style acting and controversy reverberating louder than the canned laughter—but a whole slew of "think" comedies were premiering left and right. Remembering CBS's initial interest in a family sitcom that would realistically explore the generation gap, Alan and his friend Marc Merson put their heads together and came up with *We'll Get By*.

It premiered on March 14, 1975, starring Paul Sorvino as George Platt, an attorney living in the New Jersey suburbs with his wife Liz (Mitzi Hoag) and their teenage children. The geographical setting was a slice of Alan's own life, and the everyday crises of the Platt family were based in part on crises that the Aldas had faced and survived in raising their own children. Daughter Andrea (Devon Scott) wore braces and hid in her upstairs room, where she read philosophy and poetry and worried that fate would play a gruesome trick on her and keep her adolescent all her life. The Platts' two sons Muff (Jerry Hauser) and Kenny (Willie Aames) anguished over homework, peer pressure, slave-wage allowances and parents who seemed exasperatingly oblivious to their deepest needs.

Of course, the entire show wasn't a photographic replica of Alan's own family life, although George and

Liz shared a common bond with Alan and Arlene as concerned, supportive parents. Liz was a lot quieter and more acquiescent than Arlene Alda, although she generally turned out to be the truth-sayer in many episodes. George, on the other hand, was more blustery and emotional than Alan and constantly worried about his weight. That bit of characterization may actually have come from an earlier part of Alan's life, before he slimmed down as a teenager.

On the basis of the pilot, CBS agreed to air ten episodes of *We'll Get By* as a 1975 midseason replacement show. Alan wrote six of the scripts himself and supervised and edited the four remaining scripts. The series aired on Friday nights from 8:30 to 9:00 P.M., a time slot that CBS had had trouble filling all season. The previous fall, CBS had televised *Planet of the Apes* from 8:00 to 9:00 P.M. on Friday nights, but the video version of the hit movie got clobbered by ABC's *Six Million Dollar Man* and NBC's *Chico and the Man*. Unfortunately, *We'll Get By* didn't do much better. It stayed on the air for only ten weeks and fell by the wayside on May 30, 1975.

The shame of it was that *We'll Get By* was an excellent program—thoughtful, intelligent, yet heartwarming and entertaining at the same time. But viewers never had a chance to get to know the show before it was canceled. As a case in point, *Barney Miller*, which premiered on ABC in January 1975, also got off to a slow start in the ratings—and Hal Linden was no more or less known to TV audiences than Paul Sorvino. But ABC had faith in the show and kept it on the air long enough for it to find its audience. Unfortunately, *We'll Get By* got no such sensitive handling, and most of America never got to see the incredibly fine performances of Paul Sorvino and Devon Scott (who seemed to share most of the series' most poignant and compelling moments, perhaps because writing father-daughter scenes came easiest to Alan).

We'll Get By was barely off the air when Alan launched headlong into creating another television series, *Hickey vs. Anybody*. This time he tried his luck with NBC, but fared even worse. Jack Weston was cast as the title character, a lawyer constantly on the verge of bankruptcy. As Alan described Hickey, "He'll do anything to make a buck. He's not a criminal, he just has a very flexible set of ethics." NBC held the pilot for a while, then decided not to pick it up as a fall series. No one will ever know whether it was the quality of the pilot or the thinking of the network programming executives which was responsible for Hickey's hasty demise. Considering most of the shows that did make NBC's new fall lineup that season it's hard to tell. *Fay*, a situation comedy starring Lee Grant as a harried divorcée, didn't even last as long as the heroine's marriage. *The Montefuscos*, which critics nicknamed "The Waltons Italian-Style," came and went in short order, too, as did most of the cops-and-robbers series that NBC seemed particularly enamored of that season.

Alan's last assault on prime-time television, a show called *Susan and Sam* with Robert Foxworth and Christine Belford, turned out to be his third strikeout. The series focused on a news reporter and his former research girl who used to get along swell until her own career began to threaten his. As an idea for a series, it was very *au courant*. Woodward and Bernstein, the Pulitzer Prize winning Watergate investigators, had given journalism a new glamour, and male-female career conflicts were definitely on people's minds, with women rapidly moving into the labor force. But despite those pluses, *Susan and Sam* also petered out as a possible network series.

For Alan, the mid-1970s were a strange mixture of

failure and success. On the one hand, he was like King Midas when it came to M*A*S*H and everything he touched turned to gold. He was winning accolades as an actor, writer and director. And according to the "Q" ratings—the secret network polls that rank actors by their likability quotient—Alan was one of the highest-rated stars in America. But on the other hand, he was not meeting with success in his quest to establish himself as a creator and developer of new television series. As a writer, Alan began to turn his sights away from television and investigate new mediums to sell his wares.

By the later 1970s, it appeared as if the golden age of comedy was over, anyway. Mary Tyler Moore had faded into daytime reruns; *All in the Family* had lost much of its original punch; and *Mary Hartman*, perhaps the most brilliantly outrageous comedy of them all, disappeared in a sea of waxy yellow buildup. America was deep into the Jimmy Carter era now, trying to live with inflation, unemployment, hard times and a declining level of personal expectations. Realism and controversy were out; what the American television watcher wanted now, it seemed, was pure escape—frivolous fantasy, designer jeans and a reassuring return to farce and innocence. The new rage in sitcoms were shows like *Three's Company, Alice,* and *The Love Boat*—shows where everything was wrapped up neatly before the last commercial. Even drama was mild and reassuring. *Charlie's Angels* was a cuddly crime series, with an emphasis on feminine pulchritude, not violence; *Dallas* was a preposterous soap opera; and *The Incredible Hulk* and *Chips* posed no tragedy that a nine-year-old mind couldn't cope with. In an atmosphere like that, Alan wasn't sure whether he wanted to pour his creative energy into television anymore. What chance was there for an intelligent, realistic series? All three networks seemed to be turning their backs on the tremendous programming revolution they'd sparked less than ten years before. Maybe it was time for Alan to knock on the doors of the movie studios and see if the creative atmosphere there was a little less stifling.

17

During his first five seasons on *M*A*S*H*, Alan limited his work schedule entirely to television. Whatever professional time he could spare away from the grind of his weekly TV series was divided between starring on occasional prime-time specials, like *Six Rms Riv Vu*, and developing new series for the small screen, like *We'll Get By*. During the months of the year when prime-time filming shut down in Hollywood, Alan preferred lining up speaking engagements around the country to stump for his favorite cause—passage of the Equal Rights Amendment—to returning to Broadway or involving himself in moviemaking. In many ways, during the 1970s, Alan had become a rather easygoing and complacent star—treating his work on *M*A*S*H* very much as a regular, full-time job and very uninterested in pushing his career to the limits to conquer new worlds as an actor.

But by 1977, he was growing restless enough to think twice about turning down movie offers. Perhaps Alan was anxious to make his move now because suddenly he felt the ground shifting under him, professionally and personally. For starters, he was past forty, a time when men generally take stock of their lives and feel uneasy about standing still when so much of life already lies behind and too little beckons ahead. Moreover, after five years on M*A*S*H, Alan couldn't help wondering just how long the magic of doing the show would last. Even smash hit comedies don't have eternal staying power on television, and it seemed to him the time wasn't far off when Alan Alda and Hawkeye Pierce would have to go their separate ways. When the popularity of M*A*S*H ebbed—as someday it inevitably would—Alan wanted to be able to survive the show's demise, not find his own career canceled with it. He'd seen too many actors, after years in a single hit series, fade into oblivion because they didn't know how or where to find that next smart career step.

Aside from the danger of stereotyping, Alan had other reasons for wanting to rebuild his movie career. His daughters were grown now, and getting ready to go off to college; he could afford to handle more projects without cutting into family time. In fact, since the girls were old enough to fend for themselves, Arlene could leave Leonia and even join him on a movie location. And at this point, having tried and failed to interest the networks in some of his original ideas for television series, Alan felt that movies might be a more promising venture for him than prime time.

In 1977, he accepted a starring role in the screen version of *Same Time, Next Year,* the big Broadway comedy about a happily married man and a happily married woman who indulge in one extramarital fling with each other annually, for twenty-five years. During the course of the film, the two characters age poignantly together, becoming friends as well as lovers, as they share each other's joys and tragedies. In the movie, Ellen Burstyn reprised her Tony-winning role, while Alan took over for Charles Grodin, who'd been Miss Burstyn's leading man on Broadway. The film was a sizable success at the box office, although when the 1978 Oscar nominations were announced, Ellen Burstyn was in the race for best actress, while Alan's name was excluded from the actor's list (shades of *Owl and the Pussycat*).

That same year Alan also turned in a performance in the Neil Simon film *California Suite*, sharing star billing with Jane Fonda, Bill Cosby, Michael Caine and Walter Matthau. That film was also a money-maker for all concerned—and a personal critical success for British actress Maggie Smith, who claimed her second Academy Award for her performance in the movie as an actress garnering an Academy Award. Between Ellen Burstyn's nomination for *Same Time, Next Year*, and Maggie Smith's victory for *California Suite*, somebody at the 1978 Oscar telecast joked that the Academy Award rules had been changed to read, "Only actresses who appear in films with Alan Alda will be considered eligible to be nominated."

In 1979, Alan emerged as both a screenwriter and box-office star in the critically praised *Seduction of Joe Tynan*. Originally titled *The Senator*, the film was released as *The Seduction of Joe Tynan*, probably because the reigning money men at Universal felt that something a little more scintillating than simple politics had to be etched in the public mind before movie-goers would line up in droves to buy tickets. Alan wrote the script in collaboration with Richard Cohen, a Washington political journalist, but left the directing chores to Jerry Schatzberg. Schatzberg's last project, *Dandy, the All-American Girl*, starring Stockard Channing, had been shelved and never released by Metro-Goldwyn-Mayer. But once Universal teamed him with Alan Alda, M-G-M suddenly perked up and the Stockard Channing film, retitled *Sweet*

Revenge, was finally distributed to Los Angeles movie theaters.

The theme of *Joe Tynan* was seduction in a double sense. The title character, played by Alan Alda, is a liberal New York senator who winds up seduced both by power and a beautiful woman. In a key Senate battle, he compromises his principles when his vote on a controversial presidential appointment becomes crucial. At first, Tynan leads a conservative Senate leader to believe that he'll back the appointment in order to get the senator's support. Later, he votes against the appointment, wary of losing his liberal supporters. Worse yet, Joe Tynan manages to turn his stand on the issue into a massive public-relations stunt that helps launch him as a future presidential contender.

At the same time that Tynan is bending his idealism to suit his own career advancement, he's also bending his private scruples a little bit, too. As the pressures of his Washington career increasingly isolate him from his wife and children in New York, he embarks on an affair with the amoral female attorney who's serving as his Senate legal adviser.

Deeply committed to politics himself, Alan had long been intrigued by the personal lives of congressmen—the men we elevate to positions of incredible power—and the price they pay for living on a national pedestal. In a sense, he felt, the double standard was almost an inevitable escape valve for most politicians. But the actual idea for the film first began germinating in his mind during a trip to Illinois when Alan joined a woman's group campaigning for state passage of the Equal Rights Amendment. He was shocked, then disillusioned, when a well-known state legislator told a female lobbyist he'd consider voting for ERA in exchange for the key to her hotel room.

Alan worked long and hard on the script, not only

to paint a realistic picture of the tangled world of Washington politics, but also to make Joe Tynan a compelling and understandable character despite his rampant double standard. To add more layers of dimension to the film, he also gathered a superb cast of actors to flesh out the other roles. Longtime friend Barbara Harris, who'd worked comfortably with Alan many years before in New York's *Second City Revue* and *The Apple Tree*, was cast as the senator's harried wife; Meryl Streep played the ambitious, power-driven seductress, while Melvyn Douglas turned in one of the best performances of his career as the aging, senile senator whom Joe Tynan eventually double-crosses.

A major theme of the film was Tynan's constant battle to hold his family together, while diverting all his energy and enthusiasm to his career. Certainly the absentee-husband syndrome isn't the exclusive province of politicians, and Joe Tynan's downfall would have seemed no less convincing had he been a corporate tycoon, a Park Avenue lawyer or even a show-business personality like Alan himself. But Alan purposely chose to make Tynan a United States senator because, he felt, politics more than any other profession makes "putting aside family for the pursuit of ambition" a nationally accepted mode of life.

Nevertheless, the message was universal—a message that had been uppermost in Alan's mind for many years. Most of all, he wanted this film to make America realize that the traditional male ethic—the idea that a man's identity depends solely on his professional success—is just as dehumanizing as the notion that a woman's identity depends on her ability to run a home and bear children. Speaking with *Daily News* writer Patricia O'Haire, Alan emphasized that men like Joe Tynan grow up with two sets of values in our culture—family life and career—and when those drives come into conflict they usually wind up destroying the man in some way. "On the one hand," he said, "we have human value—marriage, the idea that one's family should come first. On the other is a very clear message that you should do everything you can to be successful. Obviously, the two don't mesh, and a lot of men think you can put the people you care about in limbo until you reach your area of success."

The trouble is, once you succeed, it's often too late. The inevitable outcome of the absentee-husband syndrome is a man who is a stranger to his grown children and whose only remnant of contact with his wife is the alimony check he signs every month. In *Joe Tynan*, Alan articulated the absentee-husband syndrome with shattering clarity. Tynan worked longer and longer hours in Washington until he rarely saw his family at all, except on occasional hurried weekends. While his rising Senate career demanded total concentration, it also destroyed his relationship with his wife. Totally self-involved, Tynan could only see his wife's growing estrangement as a personal desertion; so he turned to another woman for the warmth and affection he no longer found at home. That "seduction," of course, only brought him more emotional turmoil, instead of contentment.

Repeatedly, in the film, Alda begged Barbara Harris to give up her life in New York and move to Washington with him. Had she been a totally traditional character, she would have acquiesced—and obviously the film would have ended halfway through the script. But Barbara Harris' refusal to sacrifice her life and work in favor of her husband's was a special point that Alan wanted to make. It was a problem he and Arlene had worked through successfully in their own marriage. When *M*A*S*H* had taken Alan to Los Angeles, instead of uprooting the whole family, Arlene and the children had chosen to stay in Leonia, and Alan had been the one to compromise, by commuting home from the West Coast regularly to see them.

Alda the screenwriter set up the two major women in the film to embody contrasting female viewpoints. Both were career women, yet different as day and night. Barbara Harris, who played a psychologist in the film, put her work on an equal footing with her home and children. Meryl Streep, though married, was totally driven and ambitious. She lived, breathed, ate and slept politics twenty-four hours a day, and so her character shared a special interest with Joe Tynan that his wife refused to share. In Alda's own words, when Joe Tynan made love to her, he was really having "an affair with his own ambition." Yet in the end, the senator abandoned his mistress and returned to his wife. Why? Alan Alda was definitely trying to make a social statement, rarely seen in movies these days, by allowing Barbara Harris, the middle-aged wife, to triumph over Meryl Streep, the younger and more attractive "other woman." Over and over again, Alan's sympathy seems to lie with the Barbara Harrises of the world—the quiet, intelligent woman who isn't quite the traditional homemaker, but hardly the liberated free spirit who blithely foregoes everything else—marriage, children, the whole domestic scene—for the sake of professional success. She is, in this way, very much like Alan's own wife. In a sense, she is also the forgotten woman, especially on the current motion-picture scene. In recent years, Hollywood has become totally absorbed with depicting liberated career types—Faye Dunaway in *Network*, Jane Fonda in *Julia*. In *The Seduction of Joe Tynan*, Alan wanted to show that an ordinary, middle-aged woman—who may not be fashionably seductive—could ultimately emerge more appealing than a young and flashy temptress.

In his next film, *The Four Seasons*, Alan carried that theme even further with Carol Burnett's character of Kate Burroughs. Here was a confident, poised woman past forty who still enjoyed a very romantic relationship with her husband after twenty-some years of marriage. What a refreshing counterpoint to films like *An Unmarried Woman, The Turning Point* and *Starting Over*, that tried to promote the premise that once a woman passes thirty-five, divorce, frustration and neurotic relationships with men are all she has to look forward to.

The Seduction of Joe Tynan launched Alan Alda as a rising moviemaker, proving there was room at the box office for films that offered America something other than a nude Brooke Shields in *The Blue Lagoon* or tormented teenage babysitters in *When a Stranger Calls*. Ironically, despite the mature, middle-aged theme of *Joe Tynan*, the film was a particular hit among college audiences; and Alan Alda and Meryl Streep were voted Man and Woman of the Year by the Harvard Hasty Pudding Club.

In October 1979, on the heels of that success, Alan and Martin Bregman, his *Joe Tynan* producer, entered into a three-picture deal with Universal Studios, with Alan slated to star in all three efforts along with writing and directing them. Bregman, who was responsible for launching Al Pacino to super-fame in *Serpico* and *Dog Day Afternoon*, gave Alan free rein as writer and director and allowed him to cast actors he felt comfortable working with.

Their first screen project was already in Alan's typewriter when the ink was still drying on their Universal contracts, and *The Four Seasons* went into production in March 1980, as soon as Alan completed his last batch of *M*A*S*H* episodes for that season. The movie was budgeted at $20 million and shot in four locations—Vermont, North Carolina, Georgia and the

Virgin Islands. For the first time, Alan was able to bring his whole family into the project. His two younger daughters, Elizabeth and Beatrice, both took time off from college to play minor roles in the film as Alda's daughter and Len Cariou's daughter. Arlene joined the crew on location, keeping a photographic diary of the filming that she later turned into a hardcover picture book, called *On Set*, for Fireside/Simon and Schuster. And oldest daughter Eve helped her mom shoot photographs of vegetables that became an integral part of Sandy Dennis' neurotic character in the film (Sandy played a photographer who shot only vegetables).

Alan did his first draft of *The Four Seasons* on three-by-five index cards, scribbling down random ideas for characters and situations. He claims the pivotal confrontation in the film was sparked by an episode in his own life—when he learned that two of his closest friends were getting a divorce and he found himself judging instead of consoling them.

As his wife, Alan chose Carol Burnett, who had become a close personal friend after they'd made *Six Rms Riv Vu* several years before. Most of the other leads—Jack Weston, Sandy Dennis and Rita Moreno—were also friends; and Len Cariou—as Nick, the faithless husband—was an actor whose work Alan had admired on Broadway in *A Little Night Music* and *Sweeney Todd*. Newcomer Bess Armstrong, cast as Cariou's young bride, had shown a strong comic flair and a believable vulnerability on a short-lived CBS series, *On Our Own*.

Making *The Four Seasons*, the cast endured almost as many vacation agonies as the bumbling couples they played. In the Virgin Islands, Jack Weston grew more and more nervous trying to hide from the hot Caribbean sun between takes. Jack had a tendency to burn easily, and the cinematographer worried that

Jack's skin tones might not match on camera from one day to the next. Carol Burnett had to have a television set installed in her dressing trailer on every location because she absolutely refused to miss a single episode of her favorite soap opera, *All My Children*. One simple scene in the Caribbean took hours to shoot not because anyone flubbed his lines or the cameramen ran out of film but because a flock of sea gulls (obviously not members of the Screen Actors Guild) declined to cooperate. Alan wanted the gulls in the frame, but they repeatedly flew out of camera range. Finally, the prop man sent out for a pizza and sprinkled the crumbs on the water to lure the gulls back and keep them there. But that wasn't the only problem. Since the Virgin Islands sailboat sequence was shot near an actual resort, sightseers kept renting motorboats and sailing out to catch a glimpse of Alda, Burnett and company. Dozens of times film had to be scrapped because tourists, hanging over the sides of their boats and waving autograph books, had sailed right into camera range.

The Four Seasons was Alan's maiden voyage as a movie director, a far lengthier and more complicated task than directing occasional segments of *M*A*S*H*. Filming went on for three months, and it was Alan's first time out doing extensive location shooting. The cast and crew generally gave him high marks for being patient, low-keyed and sensitive to the other actors' point of view in fleshing out their own characters. Still, it was hard for Alan, both star and screenwriter, to be entirely objective when he was sitting in the director's chair. Some of the grips remarked that Alan shot far more film of scenes in which he appeared than of scenes in which he was absent from the screen. He seemed to require an excessive amount of footage of himself to make sure that he could eventually edit his own performance down to sharp perfection. The rest of the cast he let breeze through their scenes without exercising the same kind of caution. Was this an act of vanity, or simply overcompensation on Alan's part? He claimed that he needed to see more film of himself than of anyone else in the editing room because he had more trouble judging himself onscreen.

The Four Seasons was a rather daring effort in today's Hollywood terms. It was a film with no explicit sex, no violence or preoccupation with the supernatural. Instead of rock music or country-western serenades, the soundtrack reverberated to the classical strains of Vivaldi. Almost all the characters were middle-aged—men with thinning hair and slightly protruding waists; women with lined faces and lots of PTA battles behind them. Even Bess Armstrong, the only one under thirty in the whole crowd, was hardly a teenybopper, and was depicted as far more serious and intelligent than are most young women in movies.

Although The Four Seasons dealt with divorce and betrayal and growing older, the main focus was friendship—and how to survive it. New York Daily News writer Cynthia Heimel suggested, "The movie seems to be saying that even if our friends drive us nuts we should love them, cope with them, give as much as we can." Like the characters on M*A*S*H, each member of The Four Season's company came lavishly equipped with his own set of endearing, but maddening, foibles. Jack Weston was a panicky hypochondriac. His wife, Rita Moreno, yelled too much. Alan Alda refused to yell at all, which infuriated his wife, Carol Burnett, who felt constantly frustrated in trying to have a decent argument with him. Sandy Dennis preferred photographing vegetables and memorizing trivial facts to dealing head-on with human emotions; and Len Cariou, after divorcing her, ruined everyone else's vacation by bringing Bess

Armstrong along with him—and disturbing everyone's sleep with the ecstatic groans of his renewed virility. Bess Armstrong was the most annoying character of all—by virtue of being younger, prettier, and slimmer than all the other wives—and a good sport to boot. They hated her precisely because she was impossible to hate. Young women who steal middle-aged husbands are supposed to be stacked, scatterbrained and shallow. Poor Bess turned out to be bright, human and likable.

The chemistry between the actors made *The Four Seasons* a very entertaining film. Some critics scoffed and called it soap opera and sentiment, but moviegoers welcomed it with open arms. Just ten days after *The Four Seasons* opened around the country, it had already grossed over $11 million in box-office receipts, and by late summer had become one of Universal's most profitable motion pictures of 1981. In *The Seduction of Joe Tynan*, Alan had merely proved that he could make a movie; in *The Four Seasons*, he showed Hollywood that he could bring in a winner. The previous year Robert Redford had won an Academy Award for directing *Ordinary People*. Alan, in his first time out as a film director, had again demonstrated that actors have a better handle on the current moviegoing pulse than many veteran directors.

He still owes Universal two more pictures, and now all of Hollywood is waiting to see what Alan Alda, the triple-threat star, screenwriter and director, will accomplish in his next efforts. Alan isn't the first performer to craft his own scripts and edit his own films—Woody Allen and Warren Beatty undoubtedly paved the way for him—but he is the first television personality to take over the motion-picture screen in such a big way. The question is, what can Alan do for an encore after *The Four Seasons?* Warren Beatty chooses to make movies only sporadically; Woody Allen, on the other hand, churns them out as fast as other comedians invent new jokes. The trouble is that Woody, in recent years, hasn't been able to sustain the success of films like *Bananas* and *Annie Hall*. The challenge of writing, directing and acting can drain the creativity of a single human being very quickly.

As for *The Four Seasons*, Alan Alda is justly proud of this opus, not so much because it helped keep Universal in the black, but because it proved his judgment right about average American moviegoing taste. Audiences *are* willing to sit still for films that don't promote sex and violence, that feature adult actors dealing with the problems of the post-thirty-five-year-old generation.

18

According to every poll in America, Alan Alda is a man women like and respect. They admire his acting and the wholesomeness he projects both on the screen and off, and despite the fact that he lacks the ruggedness of a Robert Redford or the brooding sensuality of an Al Pacino, they consider him a very sexy man.

What women find appealing about Alan Alda is his sensitivity—and his strong stand on feminist issues underlines his basic concern for women. Alan recently donated $11,000 to help save the Seneca Falls home of Elizabeth Cady Stanton, a pioneer in the women's suffrage movement. The New York premiere of *The Four Seasons* also had feminist overtones. Ticket sales raised $60,000 for the Ms. Magazine Fund for Investigative Journalism and the magazine, in turn, devoted a thoughtful cover story to Alan to coincide with the opening of the film.

Aside from playing a financial role in the women's movement, Alan has used his star clout in other ways to support the cause. Over the years, he's turned down television scripts that he felt were offensive to women and has actively campaigned for the ratification of the Equal Rights Amendment. Alan's daughter Beatrice thinks that her father's concern stems from the fact that he's raised three girls. But Alan thinks that's nonsense. He replies that if he had sons, he'd raise them to be feminists, too.

As early as 1975, Alan was attending fundraisers to back the passage of ERA. Close friends like Marlo Thomas and Gloria Steinem helped spur his interest, but his concern actually dated back to his own childhood. His bout with polio was perhaps the strongest influence of all. Alan never forgot that Sister Elizabeth Kenny, the woman whose treatment had saved him from permanent paralysis, had been shunned by the predominantly male medical profession. Later, as a father, he wanted to make sure that his daughters wouldn't be victimized by the same kind of inequality when they grew up. He felt then, and he still feels now, that passage of the Equal Rights Amendment would assure equal pay for equal work and eliminate job discrimination and the subtle forms of sexism that exist on the employment scene.

In 1975, at a Chicago benefit for ERA, Alan told the audience, "Everybody suffers when you squash one half of the population." Sexism, he asserted, undermines marriage, because "How can you have a happy life with someone who is swatted down like a gnat?"

Why are so many men opposed to equal rights for women? Alan thinks the opposition stems from fear. They're frightened that ratification of the amendment means they'll no longer be the sole breadwinner in the family, that their wives and daughters will be eligible for military combat, and that women will be forced out of the house and pushed into competing with them on the job market. All of these fears, of course, are total misconceptions about ERA. The amendment would only make discrimination against women illegal in plain and simple terms. It would not compel women to bear arms or become truckdrivers or stop cooking dinner (unless, of course, they wanted to). But ignorance breeds fear, it seems, and this is always the greatest obstacle to social progress.

In his 1975 Chicago speech, Alan emphasized that ERA would help men as much as it would help women, freeing them from their stereotyped roles of being workhorses and protectors of women. "I think we all need to come to a new awareness of each other," he said. Men, after all, suffer from the propagation of antifeminism, too. As long as a woman's place is only in the kitchen, a man bears the whole financial and emotional brunt of supporting his family. He's indoctrinated from birth to be aggressive, ambitious and strong. Qualities like sensitivity and tenderness are considered signs of weakness—and many men go through life frustrated (and lonely, if they'd only admit it) because they're trapped on a perpetual treadmill of work, eat and sleep.

According to Alan, "Everybody stands to benefit from equality of the sexes. Our movement will free people to be as soft as they are, or as tough as they need to be to get their work done without having to conform to something which is not in them." His eloquence on the lecture circuit, combined with his instant recognition factor as a television star, soon made Alan one of the premier spokespersons for ERA in the country. President Ford appointed him as a member of a special White House commission to coodinate the observance of International Woman's Year.

In 1979, Alan himself was honored for his dedicated service to promoting women's rights. The College of Marin in California sponsored a gala tribute to Alan with two thousand guests in attendance. Gloria Steinem, who had been a friend of Alan's since 1964 when they both toiled on *That Was the Week That*

Was, served as mistress of ceremonies and introduced film clips from Alan's career. The evening's proceeds (more than $20,000) went to the Ms. Foundation, a cause close to the hearts of both the emcee and the guest of honor.

By the end of the 1970s, however, the passage of ERA still looked shaky—and even a spokesperson like Alan Alda couldn't seem to break through the barriers of fear and ignorance that kept too many states from ratifying it. Alan, of course, didn't want people to favor it simply because they liked him as a celebrity; he wanted them to accept ERA because it was a valid constitutional priority. "I'm not endorsing the ERA like soap," he told *Chicago Tribune* writer Howard Kissel. "I don't want people to vote for it because I'm cute."

Today, by Alan's own admission, passage of ERA is in a "crisis state." The original deadline for passage was 1979, but Congress granted a three-year extension to June 30, 1982. Three more states still must ratify the bill in order to make it law, and celebrities like Helen Reddy, Marlo Thomas and Valerie Harper are working harder than ever to get the message across before the deadline. In May 1981, the National Organization for Women formed a crisis committee, chaired by former first lady Betty Ford and Alan Alda, to plan a last big push for ratification. Despite the fact that Alan was already committed to a long tour of Europe and Australia to promote *The Four Seasons*, he eagerly accepted being a co-chairperson because he realized how crucial time had become.

This final ERA push, according to NOW President Eleanor Smeal, will be the biggest campaign for women's rights in American history. Rallies were scheduled in 125 cities, along with a vigil outside the White House and walkathons to raise money for the campaign. *Ms.* and other women's magazines were using their contacts in the publishing field to encourage newspaper editors to print the actual wording of the amendment, since a major obstacle to passage is the fact that too many Americans don't know exactly what the amendment says. If they did, they'd realize that the amendment in no way threatens to undermine men, women, traditional family life, or marriage. All those bugaboos are simply scare tactics promoted by opponents of the bill.

As of now, the ultimate future of ERA remains in doubt, but even more depressing for Alan have been his feminist battles right in his own home territory—television. In 1975, Alan tried to arrange a meeting between women's rights leaders and network programmers to discuss the chauvinistic outlook that pervades most television scripts. On prime-time TV (and the picture hasn't changed much six years later) most female characters are subservient to men. On crime shows, women generally get to play somebody's girlfriend or somebody's victim. On situation comedies, mothers know best, but young women are generally silly and sexy or nubile and neurotic. Made-for-television movies are perhaps the worst offenders of all. When networks do opt for women's themes, the subject matter is invariably rape or prostitution—and women are consistently depicted as being victimized by men. Furthermore, the television star structure only supports the fact that women don't get a fair shake in television. The most powerful stars on prime time are Michael Landon, Carroll O'Connor, Jack Klugman, James Garner, Larry Hagman—and Alan Alda himself. All men.

But when Alan tried to get network execs to sit down at their conference table and listen to feminist complaints, he encountered a stone wall at CBS, NBC and ABC. At each network, the response was exactly the same. The programmers were all too busy to talk, besides they'd had their fill of meeting with protest groups in the past from civil-rights leaders to gay activists. Finally, Alan gave up in despair.

Nowhere is the imbalance between male and female star power more apparent than in the annual Emmy nomination list. There are so few outstanding female dramatic actresses on television that each year it becomes more difficult to round up enough nominees for the best-actress race. Not too long ago Sada Thompson (*Family*) found herself competing with Lindsay Wagner (*Bionic Woman*) and Melissa Sue Anderson (then a child actress on *Little House on The Prairie*), a rather strange grouping of talent—and indicative of the fact that there simply weren't enough leading adult females on prime-time drama.

Of course, during the past decade, shows like *Police Woman* and *Charlie's Angels* certainly haven't been traditional cops-and-robbers escapades. But Alan hardly considers them landmarks in feminist progress. He remembers meeting with NBC executives once to discuss his pilot for *Hickey vs. Anybody* when the subject of *Police Woman* came up. Alan wondered why Angie Dickinson, the star of the show, only got to chase the criminals, while Earl Holliman (her police superior) always got to apprehend them. In fact, Holliman spent most of his time each script rescuing Angie, although she was a qualified, experienced detective. To Alan's way of thinking, *Police Woman* only reinforced the traditional misconception that girls need to be protected and rescued by boys. When he mentioned that at the conference, the NBC programmers looked at him as if he were suddenly speaking Martian. Finally, one of the execs confided that if Angie Dickinson ever physically collared a criminal and disarmed him, the show's ratings would probably drop down to the cellar.

Alan considers *Charlie's Angels* equally reactionary.

Although Kate Jackson, Farrah Fawcett, Jackie Smith and all the other angels earned millions and became superstars from their TV stint, the characters they portrayed were hardly role models for American women, although they were definitely fashion models. In a recent *Redbook* interview, Alan sarcastically joked that *Charlie's Angels* "chase crooks mainly in order to get their T-shirts wet in the swimming pool. . . . the person who is really in charge is the man on the telephone."

Women may be stereotyped as sex objects, victims and middle-aged saints, but men don't get a fair shake either. TV heroes are expected to be strong, masterful individuals with a tight rein on their emotions. Men rarely cry on prime time. They drive trucks, tote guns, perform life-and-death surgery, wear suits and make business deals, and in general do a lot more *doing* than thinking. In fact, one TV pilot that Alan submitted to a network was criticized because the male hero was too verbal. A man shouldn't talk too much, Alan was told, because women viewers will think he's weak.

19

It's an interesting commentary on our times that one of the few male characters on television who regularly chatters, gossips and suffers from fits of pique is Mork the Orkan, a visitor from another planet. This season he's even having a baby, but of course that's strictly harmless farce. In a serious vein, television still has trouble depicting men who can be sensitive and nurturing without losing their masculinity.

But sexual stereotyping isn't the only fault Alan finds with prime-time programming. The family hour is another special sore point with him. He certainly doesn't favor blatant sex and violence on television, but he is wary of the enormous network censorship that goes hand in hand with selecting programs and scripts for family viewing time. Censorship of any kind, he believes, is an infringement of the constitutional guarantee of freedom of speech. If a joke has to be edited from a television script, it can set a precedent that can lead to censoring any idea from television that's the least bit unusual or disturbing.

In 1978, Alan returned to Fordham University, his alma mater, to receive an honorary graduate degree in fine arts, and he used the occasion to declare war on the insipid state of television. Alan warned the audience, "Networks employ dozens of censors to prevent us from using language on TV that eight-year-olds might have to explain to their parents. But it's not so much what we say that teaches us as what we don't say. It's the unspoken assumptions that mold an audience." Alan also deplored the fact that the golden age of comedy—represented by shows like *The Mary Tyler Moore Show* and *All in the Family*—had deteriorated into a brass age. The brilliance was gone, the product was cheapened—shows were increasingly bland. The MTM and Norman Lear shows were soft comedies (as are *M*A*S*H* and *Barney Miller*) where the laughter was secondary to the very human complications that characters found themselves in. Now hard comedies were proliferating on the home tube—shows where pratfalls, mugging and cartoon-style mishaps dominate. The characters never expressed anything more than childish emotions, and the plots were all enunciated by Lucille Ball almost thirty years ago. "Instead of real human problems," Alan said, "television is giving us vaudeville and burlesque sketches today."

Amazingly enough, Alan—who probably has the most clout of any television performer—has been unable to make any of the networks take his case seriously. The feeling in Hollywood is that if Alan Alda can't convince the bookkeepers and slide-rule experts who run the studios, then perhaps no one can. For by anyone's system of accounting, Alan today is the highest-paid and perhaps the most valuable performer on the television scene. Conservative analysts estimate his annual *M*A*S*H* salary at over $2 million, but once residuals from *M*A*S*H* reruns and his separate fees for writing and directing episodes of *M*A*S*H* are added on, the figure probably passes the $5 million mark. Gary Deeb, the Chicago television critic, calls Alan "the champion breadwinner in TV history," followed by Carroll O'Connor, who grosses a few hundred thousand dollars less a year, and Michael Landon and Larry Hagman, who hover around the $3 million mark. To 20th Century–Fox, Alan Alda *is* M*A*S*H, and the studio allows him to renegotiate his contract every year, making no secret of the fact that M*A*S*H will permanently decamp, no matter how high the ratings stay, the year Alan decides to leave the show.

Despite the fact that he's a millionaire many times over, Alan still lives an exceedingly middle-class life, pampering himself with few luxuries. He does collect oil paintings (and will soon own three homes to hang them in), but he's far from ostentatious or extravagant. A few years ago, he was driving a rented Chevy Nova to the studio. When his wife and friends finally convinced him it was time to get a new car, he invested in a Mercedes, not because it is a Hollywood status symbol, but because the car has an excellent safety record.

At this point, Alan could easily retire from M*A*S*H and devote himself to motion-picture making. But despite the fact that each year he continues to protest, "This season will probably be my last," somehow his attachment to the show remains strong and M*A*S*H keeps churning out new episodes week after week, although it's now lasted longer than the Korean War and World War II put together. At times, there have been rumors that Alan might defect for another television venture, but even if he has occasionally been approached to switch shows and networks, he's never taken any of the offers seriously. The most persistent rumor arose in 1979 when *Los Angeles Magazine* announced that Alan was a prime candidate to replace Tom Brokaw as host of NBC's

Today Show. According to the buzz, NBC was anxious to find an actor, rather than a straight news reporter, to fill the spot, since their ABC competition, *Good Morning America,* had been successful in the ratings thanks to David Hartman's anchorship. The rumor began when Joe Bartelme, executive producer of *Today,* asked Alan to substitute for Brokaw temporarily while the latter went on vacation. Alan was intrigued with the idea at trying his hand at interviewing and feature news reporting, but had to turn the offer down because of an already overcrowded schedule. Alan later laughed at reports that NBC was negotiating with him on a permanent basis, since he was already committed to a three-picture deal with Universal.

Today, Alan's TV-Q is so high that he could probably swing any television deal he wanted if he set his mind (and agent) to it. In May 1981, *People Magazine's* Annual Readers' Poll picked him for the third year in a row as the most beloved male television star. *People* readers also voted him the celebrity they'd most like to ask home to dinner (he was a more popular choice than even Ronald Reagan or Johnny Carson). Of the readers sampled, 58 percent were women, but Alan's voting strength in the pole bridged the sex lines. Male respondents were just as enthusiastic about him, and he drew large numbers of votes from both teenagers and senior citizens. Alan's popularity is the kind of across-the-board appeal that every politician dreams of—and surprisingly enough, the *People* readers also listed Alan as the celebrity they'd most like to see enter the political arena. Obviously, the sincerity and honesty he projects to the public must account for this, since Alan's own political views are hardly in vogue these days. He's a liberal, an outspoken feminist and a vocal defender of left-of-center causes like the abolishment of capital punishment and complete freedom of speech and press. Very few established political figures feel secure enough to campaign openly for all these issues, and though the public by and large is more conservative than Alan, they'd still trust him with a seat in government. An interesting reaction.

In explaining Alan's landslide victory in the survey, the editors of *People* analyzed his appeal as "a combination of talent, just imperfect enough (and hence non-threatening) good looks and provocative underexposure, even after nine seasons in prime time." Most of all, *People* decided Alan proves that "nice guys do finish first."

What does make Alan Alda appealing? Is it that he looks wholesome and nonthreatening? Or the fact that he fights like a tiger for the issues he fervently believes in? Or a combination? Journalist Carey Winfrey recently described Alan as "one of the least macho of leading men," then noted that even if fans knew that he uses four-letter language in private (and he does) it wouldn't detract from his public image. "His strong public postures on controversial issues, particularly his support for the Equal Rights Amendment, appear only to have increased his popularity," she wrote.

Alan, of course, isn't the first performer to risk his neck and career for controversial political issues. Jane Fonda's anti-Vietnam stance and Vanessa's Redgrave's support of the PLO nearly wrecked their film careers; yet Alan's political grandstanding seems to promote, rather than undermine, his career. You could argue that America has an ingrained prejudice against politically vocal women; but perhaps a more accurate judgment would be that Alan's convictions, loud and furious though they may be, are mild compared to Fonda's or Redgrave's. He's a liberal, but hardly a radical in any sense of the word, and therefore still acceptably middle-of-the-road. If you think about it, women's rights is a far from radical issue—and over the years, Alan has publicly concentrated on themes like equal pay for equal work and human liberation rather than involving himself in more militant side issues like abortion.

Marshall McLuhan, the man who formulated the theory that the medium is the message, believes that Alan has the perfect image for television success. Television is a "cool medium," and anyone or anything that has a disturbing quality doesn't adapt well to the small screen. McLuhan told *TV Guide*'s Dwight Whitney that Alan Alda is "cryptic and low-key, which is what you have to be to be welcomed back into the living room week after week. Sammy Davis, Jr., he ain't." Yes, there is something nondisturbing about Alan. He's pleasant-looking, not devastatingly handsome, sincere but soft-spoken. It's a quality he shares with other perennial TV favorites like Johnny Carson and Dick Van Dyke.

Yet McLuhan's theory that only low-keyed men make it big on television, like most theories, has some notable exceptions. Phil Donahue is a far from tame personality. Phil delves into controversial issues (that definitely disturb viewers) and often verbally attacks his guests when he catches them trying to manipulate the truth. Edward Asner is another case in point. His TV persona of Lou Grant is a stubborn, hot-under-the-collar newsman, and offscreen Asner has drawn almost as much publicity as a fiery union organizer in the television actors' strike. Yet Asner—with a "hot" image both on screen and off—has nearly as high a likability rating as Alda himself. The same *People Magazine* poll that ranked Alan as the number-one reader favorite picked Asner as the second favorite male television star. So audience tastes may not be as low-key as McLuhan suggests.

Perhaps what Phil Donahue, Edward Asner and Alan Alda all project in common is honesty, rather than coolness. In an age when Americans find it difficult to trust their politicians (or even their doctors and lawyers), these guys who come into their living rooms week after week seem principled, fair-minded and reassuringly candid.

Not everyone, of course, is an Alan Alda fan. After the *People Magazine* poll results were announced, John Podhoretz devoted an entire column in the *Los Angeles Herald Examiner* to the baffling question of why Americans would most like to have Alan Alda over for dinner. To discuss ERA? Probably not. To bask in the brilliance of his talent and ideas? Again probably not. Podhoretz' opinion was that Alan's talent is only skin deep, but he's touched the right nerve with America by becoming the self-proclaimed spokesman of the "New Sentimentality."

What Alan has done, Podhoretz claims, in movies like *Joe Tynan* and *The Four Seasons*, is tackle sensitive themes and reduce them to the level of greeting-card messages. The problems of career vs. marriage, infidelity, and midlife crisis are all laudable subjects for motion pictures, but Alan the screenwriter has made them palatable to the American public by turning them into sugar-coated soap-opera conflicts. Podhoretz felt that in *The Four Seasons* the ideas are generally cut down to the level of an eleven-year-old viewer and when Alan really wants to drive the idea home, he cuts to a closeup of Carol Burnett for a warm and wise reaction shot. After seeing *The Four Seasons*, does anyone really have a new insight into marriage and friendship and the anguish of middle age? No, they've wept a little and laughed a lot, but the effect of the film wears off quickly. It's much like watching *Dallas*, an engrossing entertainment that gives you no real idea how the oil business is run or how people in the Southwest truly live.

Above and beyond the superficiality of Alan's film scripts, Podhoretz finds Alan's image of "sensitive masculinity" a complete washout. "He radiates inoffensiveness and an odd asexuality," the critic wrote. "He looked ridiculous when called upon in *The Seduction of Joe Tynan* to demonstrate sexual passion for Meryl Streep, because Alan Alda kissing anyone except in friendship is unthinkable." Podhoretz then speculates that *Four Seasons* was probably a bigger box-office hit than *Joe Tynan* because it contained a lot of friendship kissing, and no French kissing whatsoever.

Attacks like these are inevitable, because Alan, after all, has promoted himself so widely as the new breed of thoughtful, sensitive, liberated man. *Saturday Night Live* recently took a hilarious swipe at him. The skit took place in a singles bar where a very macho guy who couldn't get a girl to give him a second glance suddenly blossomed into a ladykiller. His success was due to his taking the bartender's advice and reading Alan Alda's new sensitivity book (titled something like "How to Become a Wimp and Get Girls in Only Six Weeks"). Instead of telling girls about his waterbed or his sports achievements, his opening line now became "I'm absolutely devastated by my divorce and I desperately want to have a child." Suddenly, every girl in the bar couldn't wait to get into bed and comfort him.

Aside from the Podhoretz article and the *Saturday Night Live* satire, Alan recently cropped up as a contestant in a *New York Daily News* contest, where readers had to choose the ten celebrities they were most bored with. Nevertheless, his defenders remain as loyal as ever. Beverly Stephen rhapsodized over the appeal of Alan Alda in a recent article for the *Los*

Angeles Times. Her opening line was: "Please, God, don't ever let Alan Alda get divorced." Then she asserted that the women's movement could survive anything—even Billie Jean King's lesbian revelations—but if Alda's perfect marriage ever broke up, feminism might never recover from the fallout. She quipped that women don't want to hear anything bad about Alan. A rumor that Alan had been unfaithful to Arlene or had reneged on a promise to show up for Parents' Day at college would be like learning there was no Santa Claus. In closing her tribute to "the perfect new man," Miss Stephen admitted that Alan may not be 100 percent godlike, but he's more of a real man than most other celebrities on the Hollywood scene. "He still looks pretty good," she wrote, "still the closest thing we've got to a new male role model—a replacement for John Wayne if you will."

What would probably shock his adoring public most is the fact that the real Alan Alda can rage, fume and stomp his feet just like ordinary people. His personality is certainly low-keyed, but the women's magazines have created such an aura of unflappable dignity around him that it's hard to believe he can reach a boiling point just like anyone else. Yet he can. In May 1981, Alan and his wife and daughters all appeared at the New York Lincoln Center Library for a gala fundraiser to support the Ms. Magazine Fund for Investigative Journalism. For the press, it was a rare opportunity to photograph the entire Alda clan, but just before the cameras started clicking Alan angrily demanded that one photographer be removed from the room. The man was Ron Gallela (the same paparazzo who once harassed Jackie Onassis until she finally got a court injunction to stop him).

Alan was still fuming over an incident that had happened a year earlier when Gallela had accidentally stepped on his daughter's foot while trying to snap

Alan. Now Alda marched right up to Gallela at the Lincoln Center party and ordered him to get out. Gallela reminded Alan that he'd already made a public apology for the earlier instance and that he was only trying to do his job as a photographer. (The Lincoln Center party, after all, was a press gathering—and Gallela certainly wasn't invading the Alda family's privacy.) Ron told Alan he considered their previous hassle "all water under the bridge," but Alan refused to calm down. He said, "I don't like you. I don't like what you do. Either you go or I call the police!" Gallela got the message and left.

Even more surprising is Alan's long-running feud with former *M*A*S*H* director Jackie Cooper. During the show's first two seasons, Cooper directed a substantial portion of the segments and even won an Emmy for his direction of a 1974 episode called "Carry On, Hawkeye." The script dealt with a viral epidemic that felled the entire medical unit except for Hawkeye, leaving him on round-the-clock surgical duty until his bleary eyes couldn't distinguish a ruptured spleen from a ragged hangnail. Perhaps Cooper was able to direct this episode with such brilliance because the idea of Alan Alda in charge was a condition he lived with every day on the *M*A*S*H* set.

In his autobiography, *Please Don't Shoot My Dog*, Jackie Cooper blasts Alan as "a contradictory personality. He projects warmth and wit and wisdom, intelligence and stability. Actually, in my opinion, he is concealing a lot of hostility beneath the surface." Cooper, who'd been a Hollywood child star in the early 1930s and later a major television personality on *The People's Choice* and *Hennessey*, claims he had numerous differences with Alan over who would be in control on the set. As director, Cooper should have been in charge of the camera crew, but he claims that Alan was jealous of the crew's loyalty to Cooper. Rumor also has it that Alan was piqued by all the publicity that Jackie Cooper received during the show's first season on the air. Yet that publicity was far from unreasonable, considering the state of Alan's career at the time. In 1972, Alan was hardly a major television personality, and viewers who hadn't seen him in *Paper Lion* or *Jenny* were hardly aware of who he was. It was only natural that the Hollywood press would devote lots of newspaper space to Jackie Cooper, who'd been a major Hollywood name for forty years. Although he only worked behind the scenes on *M*A*S*H*, the very fact that he'd switched career gears from acting to directing was important news in itself.

Alan, however, claims that the feud was entirely on the other fellow's part. He labeled Cooper's references to him in his autobiography as "a bunch of distortions and half-truths," but refused to answer Cooper's charges jibe for jibe because he preferred to remain a gentleman in print, even if Cooper had lapsed on that score. Alan, however, couldn't resist getting in at least one ungentlemanly barb—namely that Cooper was dredging up their eight-year-old feud because Alan Alda's name would help sell copies of the autobiography. Still, Alan claimed he wasn't angry at Jackie anymore and couldn't understand why Jackie was still furious enough to keep firing away at him in public. Alan's response seemed to be that all he'd ever done was criticize some of Cooper's choices as a director, which is, after all, the prerogative of a conscientious actor.

Yet for all his refusal to trade verbal blows with Jackie Cooper, Alan's single jibe at the man does seem particularly snide. Whether or not Jackie Cooper was difficult to work with, or even tyrannical as a director, he didn't simply call a press conference eight years after the fact to stir up old antagonisms toward Alan. He printed this feud (granted, only his side of it) in his autobiography. What happened between Alan and Jackie on the set of M*A*S*H is definitely a valid part of the man's life, no matter how long ago it occurred. Certainly such a staunch defender of constitutional liberties as Alan would hardly want to encourage another man to censor his own autobiography. Furthermore, the very nature of an autobiography makes the writing of it a one-sided affair. That, after all, is why unauthorized biographies exist—to give the public a chance to view celebrities in as objective a light as the author can manage. People writing about themselves have a more difficult task to remain objective.

And the fact remains that Jackie Cooper, despite his Emmy win, left M*A*S*H after two seasons, while Alan stayed and gradually became one of the show's leading directors himself. Eventually, even Larry Gelbart and Gene Reynolds, the original producers, left (and associate producer Burt Metcalfe took over the reins)—although both Gelbart and Reynolds strenuously maintained that boredom, a built-in danger on any long-running series, was the sole reason for their departure. Nevertheless, some observers maintain that once Gelbart and Reynolds left, it became easy for Alan to take more and more control of the show with the power to make script revisions, okay casting choices and more and more steer the show away from comedy into serious, dramatic issues.

According to some people who have worked sporadically on the M*A*S*H set, Alan is "aloof and highly critical"—a star who wants things done in his own fashion, who controls episodes even when another director is in charge and the script has been written by someone else. Believing that M*A*S*H can only survive as long as Alan Alda stays with the show, the studio and network seem eager to back him to the hilt creatively.

These days, of course, Alan is in an enviable position professionally. After ten seasons, M*A*S*H continues to outrank many newer shows in the weekly Nielsen ratings, earning enormous profits for both CBS and 20th Century–Fox. That makes him an extremely valuable player to begin with. And with his latest movie, *The Four Seasons*, he's established the same kind of motion-picture clout as Robert Redford and Warren Beatty. He's an actor who's bankable enough to make his own independent production deals and switch-hit as screen writer and director, when he chooses to.

There are those who call him pompous and arrogant. There are also those who say Alan's just a sweet guy—a nice man trying to go about his business in Hollywood and protect himself in a very cutthroat profession, which isn't easy. Another source suggests that Alan may inadvertently alienate people because he's a lot brighter than some of the programmers and executives he comes into contact with. "Intelligence is always suspect," this source maintains, "and in Hollywood it's a particularly dangerous commodity."

Show-business veteran Joey Adams, who has known Alan Alda since childhood and whose friendship with Alan's father dates back forty years, thinks Alan is possibly one of the most misunderstood celebrities in show business today. Misunderstood in the sense that everyone is now trying to unravel the supposed complexities of Alan Alda's personality—and yet Alan, at heart, is a very simple man. He's concerned about his wife, his children and his work, and he's touched by the same humanitarian impulses that most thoughtful people share. "He's the genuine article," says Joey. "There's nothing phony or pretentious about him. He married a nice Jewish girl from the Bronx, and he loves her and he loves his work."

20

"I never wanted to be famous. The fact is I never cared for it. But I realized that if I wanted to get good acting parts and work with talented people I respected, I'd have to be well-known."

Over and over again, Alan Alda has said that; and after a decade of being in the television limelight he still cringes when phrases like "superstar" and "the most powerful man in prime time" are attached to the bits and pieces of Hollywood news that are constantly written about him.

He grows uncomfortable when journalists ask him how it feels to be a forty-five-year-old sex symbol—and he tries to joke the question off by retorting that he must be sexy; after all, he's the father of three children. He doesn't go out of his way to do talk shows or court the press, unless he has a new movie to unveil; and then he plunges into a frantic round of public exposure like a man telling his dentist, "Doc, drill all my cavities at once and just get it done." In 1979, he launched a major publicity blitz to coincide with the release of *The Seduction of Joe Tynan*. He followed much the same procedure with *The Four Sea-*

sons. The month the film premiered, Alan's face was simultaneously splashed on the covers of *People, McCall's, Ladies' Home Journal* and *Ms.* Practically every major newspaper carried a brand-new interview with Alan—and for once his wife Arlene was pictured prominently with him. She was, after all, an integral part of *The Four Seasons,* too, since her behind-the-scenes photographs of the film had been turned into a book. So speaking with the press was really a joint venture to promote both their successes.

Alan has always viewed publicity the way corporate executives view interoffice memos—a necessary part of the business, but something to be gotten out of the way as quickly as possible. Perhaps because basically it is drudgery to him, most magazine and newspaper articles written about Alan have a mechanical, repetitive slant. The lead paragraph talks about Alan's latest film or television project; a brief biographical profile follows mentioning the *Owl and the Pussycat, The Apple Tree,* and the fact that he's Robert Alda's son; then comes the part about his happy (despite all the show-business odds) marriage; and, of course, an elaborate discussion of his support of women's rights.

Has Alan Alda nothing new or provocative to say? Or is the blandness really the result of the fact that for all his outward charm and lighthearted banter Alan Alda remains an aloof man—an illusive personality that only his closest intimates ever really glimpse?

Illusiveness, it seems, is the one quality he shares with his famous father, for all the fact that their lives turned out to be such a contrast in style and temperament. On the NBC soap opera *Days of Our Lives,* where Robert now plays Stuart Whyland, castmates report that he's charming and affable, but the setside socializing rarely carries over after work. Robert prefers to go home to his wife Flora and stay close to just a few longtime friends, just as Alan avoids the bistro-and-party scene in favor of home and family.

In the years since Alan's star has ascended, Robert has mellowed and toned down considerably. His marriage to Flora Marino, which made newspaper headlines in 1957, has turned out to be an enduring and devoted match. As newlyweds, they hopscotched from one continent to another—living temporarily in New York, Los Angeles and Europe wherever Bob had a film or stage commitment. In 1959, they settled in Italy, where Bob churned out fifteen movies in a row; then in 1963; they returned to New York with their son Antony while Bob starred on Broadway in *What Makes Sammy Run?* In 1972, when Alan was emerging as a television star on *M*A*S*H*, Bob wasn't on hand to share his son's triumph, because he and Flora were living in Italy again; but two years later they returned to Los Angeles, where they've stayed ever since. Altogether, they've had about twenty homes in twenty-seven years, but now they agree that their roots are in Pacific Palisades. So, while Alan Alda remains an Easterner at heart, his father has turned out to be the full-fledged Californian in the family. Everything that makes Alan slightly uncomfortable about California living, Bob and Flora find immensely enjoyable—the slow pace, the greenery, the warm and relaxing climate. Perhaps Bob and Flora are so enchanted by the West Coast because it reminds them of Italy, where some of their happiest memories are.

Although Bob's parents were Italian, he was born and raised in New York, and in some ways marrying Flora was a bit of a culture shock. The first thing he discovered was that he and his bride didn't really speak the same language. "I grew up speaking a New York dialect of Italian," he says, "which is a combination of a lot of Italian dialects—Sicilian, Neopolitan, northern Italian—since New York immigrants came from all different parts of the old country. When I actually lived in Italy, I realized my dialect wasn't quite any version of the native language at all."

Bridging the language barrier was an education for them both. Over the years, Bob became fluent in Italian while Flora's command of American-style English more than kept pace. Today, they laugh happily that they're able to argue in two languages at once. "Flora and I both have good tempers," Bob admits, "because we have strong personalities. But I think that's healthy for a marriage. The strangest thing is that all we ever argue about is my work. Flora worries that I don't relax enough. Actually, for the first ten years we were married, we never had a bad word. People used to look at us and say, 'Are they for real?' Now when we fight, it lasts five minutes and we clear the air. We never hold a grudge."

Bob and Flora's son, Antony, is twenty-four years old now and happily married too. His wife, Lori, is a minister's daughter whom he met in Columbus, Ohio. Antony, an aspiring actor, has guest-starred on *M*A*S*H* (along with Robert) and currently has a TV pilot called *Homerun* on the drawing board at Paramount. It seems as if all the Alda men are attracted to creative women, and Lori has her own career as a professional singer.

In raising his younger son, Bob followed the same tack that he took with Alan—not actively discouraging him from entering show business, but keeping a hands-off policy, letting him take his own spills and falls, so success would be entirely his own accomplishment. Of course, Robert Alda was hardly the same man raising each of his sons, since they came into his life twenty years apart. Aside from the generation gap between the boys (Alan's daughter Eve is almost as old as Antony), Antony had the benefit of being raised in a secure, two-parent environment, while Alan's family was torn apart by the time he was a teenager.

Bob was already in his forties, and a little less driven about his own success, by the time his second son came along. It was perhaps easier for him to be a full-time father. "Having Antony kept me feeling young," he says. "Raising him, in some ways, was less of a strain because I'd been through the mill before. I knew what teething and temper tantrums and chickenpox were. I suppose my muscles ached a little more when I played baseball with him, but all in all it was fun becoming a father again past forty."

According to Flora—who can only judge Bob's relationship with Antony—he was always a warm and loving father. And certainly Bob never let show business shut him off from his younger son. In 1970, when Bob and Flora moved to Italy for four years so that he could make movies, Antony went with them and enrolled in the Notre Dame International School, a school for American kids living abroad.

Although they're half brothers, Alan and Antony bear a strong physical resemblance, since both favor their father in looks, smile and mannerisms. Their voices are so similar that when family friends phone, they often mistake Bob for Antony or Alan.

Bob and Flora still consider themselves religious, although, as for Alan and Arlene, their faith is a very private matter. In recent years, Flora has become interested in yoga and meditation; occasionally Bob has gone to the lectures with her, but he admits he enjoys listening to someone talk about the benefits of yoga far more than actually practicing it himself. Flora, though, attends a self-realization center near their Pacific Palisades home; it's a meditative group that welcomes people of all religions.

Unlike Alan and Arlene, the elder Aldas have only a casual interest in the women's liberation movement; and obviously heated discussions must arise when Alan, Arlene and their daughters spend Christmas and Thanksgiving at Bob's house. Flora voluntarily gave up her European acting career at the time she married Bob; that was twenty-seven years ago, and she claims she's never had a moment's regret. "She was getting a little tired of her career anyway," Bob says. "Before we got married, we talked about it and decided that with my career in America and hers in Italy, both of us working would be a ridiculous complication. We'd never get together, and there's always the danger of ego clashes when both spouses are actors. Why should we have to face that? Financially, I knew I could take care of us and any children that might come along. It was something we saw eye to eye on."

As for liberation, a cause that is so close to his son's heart, Bob has rather dubious feelings. "I always felt I was liberated as a man," he says. "Liberated is such a loosely used word today. Flora and I have been getting along very well all these years, and neither of us is playing a role."

Flora does support the Equal Rights Amendment—believing women should get equal pay for equal work—but she believes a truly equitable relationship between a man and a woman is a matter of the heart, not the law. "If a man treats you like a queen, you treat him like a king," she says, smiling warmly at her husband.

"The liberation comes automatically," Bob agrees. "You don't look for it, it's there."

Flora wonders what the eventual outcome of too much liberation might be, and thinks society will suffer if women abandon their roles of mothers and homemakers en masse. "I can't believe wives who are *never* home," she exclaims. "Who's taking care of the house? Who's raising the children? I call friends and the wives are never there."

But recently Flora found a way to stay home and embark on an adventurous project, in much the way that her daughter-in-law Arlene has done. With Bob, she co-authored a best-selling cookbook, *99 Ways to Cook Pasta*, a collection of recipes culled from their own families and from the kitchens of various world-famous restaurants they've patronized over the years.

The cookbook was actually Bob's idea, but he encouraged Flora to do the writing and recipe testing as a way to fill up her time when he was working on the NBC nighttime series *Supertrain*. Bob was spending twelve-hour days at the studio, and he feared that Flora would grow bored and lonely, especially since Antony was no longer at home. Bob happened to be at a party in New York when he ran into Toni LaPopola, an editor at Macmillan, whom he'd known since she was a little girl. As a youngster Toni used to tag along with her family when they visited Bob's house in the San Fernando Valley during his Warner Brothers stint. She never forgot the delicious Italian pasta dishes he had whipped up for guests. When they met in New York, Toni's first question was, "Do you still make those terrific meatballs and spaghetti?" Bob laughed and said he didn't cook anymore because he had an Italian wife who was the real chef in the family. Then he told Toni about his cookbook idea, and she later flew out to Los Angeles to persuade Flora to collaborate with Bob on the project. By the time the book went to press, it had become a real family affair. Alan wrote the introduction and Arlene photographed the dishes to illustrate the recipes.

Ironically, as a bride, Flora was a less than adequate cook. She came from a well-to-do family where servants prepared most of the meals, so she never learned the first thing about straining linguini. As newlyweds, she and Bob dined out a lot, but when Antony was an infant, they began staying home most nights and one day Flora simply told herself, "Today, you are going to attack the kitchen!"

It took Bob and Flora eighteen months to finish the manuscript for their complete guide to pasta. Flora researched recipes from her mother and sister, Bob unearthed a few specialties from his own family, and they contacted the owners of restaurants who allowed them to print the recipes of some of their most memorable dishes. Flora also invented new dishes herself, while they wrote the book. All that pasta-straining and writer's cramp was worth it. The public not only developed a healthy appetite for the recipes in the book but *99 Ways to Cook Pasta* won a publishing award during its first year in print.

While Robert and Flora basked in the glow of their publishing success, Alan continued to whip up his own recipe for success. Shortly before he began filming a record tenth season of *M*A*S*H*, Alan threw his travel clothes together and Arlene packed up her camera equipment for a whirlwind tour of Australia, New Zealand, and Europe. The trip, ostensibly, was to promote the international release of *The Four Seasons* in foreign movie markets, but for Alan and Arlene it was a kind of delayed second honeymoon as well. They'd waited an awfully long time to squeeze this "great escape" into their busy schedules.

Just before leaving the United States, the "newlyweds" (soon to celebrate their silver anniversary) touched down briefly in New York for a reunion with their treasured friend, Marlo Thomas. Again, it was a happy case of mixing business with pleasure. Alan and Marlo were in New York to tape a Home Box Office special for cable television. The show, entitled *She's Nobody's Baby*, chronicled the saga of the twentieth-century American woman—from the Gibson Girl era to World War II's "Rosie the Riveter," the 1950s' suburban golfing wife and the 1970s' liberated feminist. Cohosting the documentary (which was produced by *Ms.* Magazine), Alan and Marlo took turns narrating the magazine-style segments.

The HBO special was taped in mid-August, and the Aldas set the rest of the summer aside for fun and travel. But in Europe and Australia, the pace didn't let up. If Alan thought he could forget the pressures of stardom for a while, he was sadly mistaken. Overseas, fans rushed to greet him everywhere he went. For the first time, Alan became aware that he is now truly an international star. His charming style of comedy and sensitivity no longer belongs to America alone. The Alda magic is a beloved commodity to millions of people all over the world.

But even if he couldn't become anonymous for a while halfway across the world, Alan truly enjoyed the trip. After a decade of almost nonstop work—acting, writing, directing, and lecturing—suddenly it was refreshing to be a carefree tourist; Alan might gladly have extended his vacation except for pressing commitments at home. In October he was due back in Los Angeles, not only to report for medical duty on *M*A*S*H* but to accept a very special tribute from the National Conference of Christians and Jews. On October 15th Alan was honored at a lavish fund-raising dinner at the International Ballroom of the Beverly Hilton Hotel. There he received the organization's Humanitarian Award, an honor previously bestowed on the likes of Jack Benny, Carol Burnett, Bob Hope, and Charlton Heston. This award, given by the NCCJ's Entertainment Industries Division, is considered one of the highest accolades Hollywood has to offer.

* * *

Now settling comfortably into his forty-sixth year, it seems as though Alan is at the zenith. His earliest ambition—as recorded in his high-school yearbook—was simply to follow in the footsteps of his famous father. Alan Alda has done that, and much more. Professionally, many years of success undoubtedly lie ahead of him. While his television triumphs are already memorable, on the motion-picture scene he has merely scratched the surface of his talent. In the next decade, he will probably write and direct even finer screenplays.

No one is prouder of Alan and his success—as actor, husband, father, and man—than Robert Alda. Certainly they are not Hollywood's first case of two-generation stardom, nor will they be the last. But Alan and Robert Alda remain a unique pair of family entertainers nonetheless. True, they are radically different personalities, but they have both conducted their lives—and careers—with style and integrity, no matter what the struggle, no matter what the challenge. Cliché it may be, but they have proven that nice guys *do* finish first.

About the Author

JASON BONDEROFF is the Editorial Director of *Daytime TV* magazine, and the author of a number of celebrity biographies, including BARBARA WALTERS, DONAHUE!, and BROOKE. He lives with his wife and two children in White Plains, N.Y.